Behind the Stained Glass

A History of
Sixteenth Street Baptist Church

The Rev. Dr. Christopher M. Hamlin

CRANE HILL
PUBLISHERS

Published by
  Crane Hill Publishers
  3608 Clairmont Avenue
  Birmingham, AL 35222
  www.cranehill.com

Printed in the United States of America

Library of Congress Cataloging-in-Publication Data

Hamlin, Christopher M.
Behind the stained glass: a history of Sixteenth Street Baptist Church/
Christopher M. Hamlin.
p.   cm.
Includes bibliographical references and index.
ISBN 1-57587-075-4   1-57587-083-5 (alk. paper)
1. Sixteenth Street Baptist Church (Birmingham, Ala.)—History.
2. Civil rights—Alabama—Birmingham—History. I. Title.
BX6480.B527H36 1998
286'.1761781—dc21   98–11543
                                                              CIP

10   9   8   7   6   5   4   3   2   1

Dedicated to Elizabeth Ann Dixie Hamlin,
who continues to offer a strong shoulder,
a challenging voice for consideration,
and a compassionate love that is unconditional,

to Doris Vivian Cornelius Hamlin, my mother,
and Fannie Belle Maymon Dixie, my mother-in-law,

to the memory of four young ladies, who came to Sunday School
on September 15, 1963, to learn about "A Love that Forgives,"

Addie Mae Collins
Denise McNair
Carole Robertson
Cynthia Wesley

to the memory of two young men, playing in the streets
of Birmingham on September 15, 1963,

Johnny Robinson
Virgil Ware

and to the memory of Christopher Maurice Hamlin II,
never held but deeply moved by his being if only for a little while,
and to Kyle Patric Hamlin, God's gift in the midst of uncertainty.

TABLE OF CONTENTS

● ● ● ● ● ●

ACKNOWLEDGMENTS
● ● ● ● ● ●

This story was first nurtured in an academic environment and mushroomed into an opportunity to highlight the 125th anniversary of a historic Birmingham institution that is dear to my heart. I could not have made an effort to share this story without the help and prayers of many people who offered themselves as buffers to the process. I am indebted to my wife and son, Elizabeth and Kyle, for their constant love and abiding faith. They add much strength to my weaknesses.

I am also indebted to Doris Vivian Cornelius Hamlin and Herman Henry Hamlin Sr., my parents, and Herman Henry Jr., Vivian Renee, Ricardo Mondel, and Kimberly Elaine, my siblings, whose struggle for light at the end of a long tunnel encourages us today. To my best friends Calvin and Sandra Birdiett and Harry and Deidra Riggs, whose voices of reason and loving care were always encouraging.

I am indebted to the late Rev. Dr. Samuel DeWitt Proctor, the Rev. Dr. Otis Moss, and the mentees of the last Moss/Proctor Fellows of United Theological Seminary, Dayton, Ohio. Dr. Proctor's keen understanding of the Black Church and the history of African Americans helped crystallize the scope of this project.

I am grateful to Sixteenth Street Baptist Church for accepting me as their pastor on January 7, 1990, and for the freedom to be free. Special words of thanks to a committed church staff: Valerie Lee, Wesley S. Halliburton, Richard Charles Young, Myrtle C. Whetstone, Ruth Mae Hawkins, Carlton Wright, and Russell Lee. I also extend my gratitude to the Rev. Dr. Rodney Franklin, the Rev. Dr. Roger Lovette, and the Rev. Dr. Karnie Smith, true friends and brothers.

The Rev. Robert Wiltshire, a new friend on the journey, helped in understanding the larger scope of Sixteenth Street Baptist Church's role in our global community. Lastly, I am appreciative to Ellen Sullivan, Norma McKittrick, and my friends at Crane Hill Publishers for their professional and caring spirit that nurtured this process from beginning to end.

Above all, I am grateful to a compassionate God in whose care I have found warmth, protection, and affirmation. May this work and all my days be a witness to the spirit that frees all humanity.

INTRODUCTION
by
The Honorable Andrew Young
● ● ● ● ● ●

In *Behind the Stained Glass: A History of Sixteenth Street Baptist Church*, the Rev. Dr. Christopher Hamlin depicts with clarity and color the events leading to that tragic day in September 1963 when a bomb killed four little girls in the church's basement in Birmingham, Alabama. The Reverend Hamlin delivers a rich history of Sixteenth Street Baptist Church, which was organized in 1873 as the First Colored Baptist Church of Birmingham. He takes us through the raucous and joyous 1940s and on into the 1960s, when the Rev. Dr. Martin Luther King's words filled the hearts of the hundreds who thronged to Birmingham to hear his message of nonviolent civil disobedience. The author leads us to that tumultuous Sunday in September 1963 and the pain of the bombing and the death of those four young black girls—and to the subsequent resurrection of the church to what it is today, not only a museum but a house of worship where God's work is done by those who love him.

This is not just a history book. It is a labor of love by someone who has found his home as the pastor and caretaker of Sixteenth Street Baptist Church, where the cries of children have been replaced by the handiwork of many of God's children.

IN MEMORY OF

DENISE MC NAIR   CYNTHIA WESLEY   ADDIE MAE COLLINS   CAROL ROBERTSON

THEIR LIVES WERE TAKEN BY UNKNOWN PARTIES ON SEPTEMBER 15, 1963 WHEN THE SIXTEENTH STREET BAPTIST CHURCH WAS BOMBED.

"MAY MEN LEARN TO REPLACE BITTERNESS AND VIOLENCE WITH LOVE AND UNDERSTANDING"

PROLOGUE

• • • • • •

Being thoroughly convinced that God does order the steps of people who offer themselves as servants, it seems that all my days, to this moment, have prepared me to pastor Sixteenth Street Baptist Church. Since 1990 I have engaged in helping our congregation understand that our ministry at Sixteenth Street Baptist Church is unique. We are discussing and trying to answer such questions as: Why is this church known worldwide, and how do we need to appropriate that knowledge into our daily ministry? Why do so many people visit our facility, and what is our responsibility toward them? Have we really earned the name "Everybody's Church"?

Examining the history of our church, how its growth paralleled that of the City of Birmingham, its open-door policy of welcoming the community to use its facility for various events, and the impact of the Civil Rights Movement, it is easy to conclude that the role of Sixteenth Street Baptist Church is more than just being a congregation of Christians worshiping in a facility. From our strategic location in downtown Birmingham, we have attempted for 125 years to be part of the strength as well as a source of change in a community that has been characteristically racist.

When segregation raised its ugly head through Jim Crow laws, Sixteenth Street Baptist Church and other institutions in the Birmingham black community found themselves being called upon to provide inspiration, training, community forums, and sources of encouragement that enabled people to say, "Ain't going to let nobody turn me round!" Knowing that a segment of society was tired of being mistreated and unfairly ostracized from the mainstream, Sixteenth Street Baptist Church opened its doors for mass meetings and strategy sessions with Dr. Martin Luther King Jr., the Rev. Fred L. Shuttlesworth, the Rev. Ralph Abernathy, the Rev. James Bevel and his wife, the Rev. Andrew Young, Dorothy Cotton, Lola Hendricks, and so many others who gave themselves as agents of change in Birmingham.

The bomb that exploded at Sixteenth Street Baptist Church on Sunday, September 15, 1963, blasted the face of Jesus Christ out of the stained-glass rose window and took the lives of four young ladies.

The critical year of the Birmingham Civil Rights campaign was 1963, and it was filled with both very positive events and gruesome nightmares. The city's black citizens showed outstanding courage in committing themselves to marching, protesting, being fired upon with high-powered fire hoses, and being arrested by Eugene "Bull" Connor. Many of these "foot soldiers" testify that they did not fully understand what they were doing at the time but they knew it was important to be involved. Their involvement provided the people power that was necessary for mass demonstrations to be effective.

The negative aspects of the Birmingham Civil Rights Movement involved police brutality and bombings. Approximately fifty-five bombings occurred in the city during that period, but none caused death until September 15, 1963, when a bomb exploded at Sixteenth Street Baptist Church and killed four young ladies. The bomb's explosion also injured twenty-two other people and caused substantial damage to our facility.

Sixteenth Street Baptist Church has been singled out for a variety of reasons. Some people see it as a unique architectural structure. Others see it as a powerful statement of the commitment of people who sacrificially gave of themselves to construct this facility, a major undertaking for blacks in Birmingham in 1909. Still others see it as a symbol of the hope and survival the congregation has provided for Birmingham's citizens during difficult times. I see the stones of this facility as symbols of the ability of oppressed people to rise above their oppression and produce something of great merit and strength.

I have always been fascinated with the power and influence of the Black Church. Growing up in Macon, Georgia, I saw firsthand as a child that there were stark differences between white and black people in the segregated South of the 1960s. The differences were noticeable in residential patterns, employment, education, public accommodations and transportation, social settings, and politics. The lines of demarcation were obvious even to my young eyes. My earliest recollection that affirmed something was wrong was when I got on a bus in Bibb County and saw a sign separating white and black people. That sign forced me to see the reality of the times, even as a young kid.

In the midst of such blatant discrimination, the Black Church provided a haven of rebirth, reconciliation, and reclaiming a freedom in God. In this institution of hope, black people transformed the midnight of disillusionment into an oasis of optimism. The Black Church offered respect and acceptance to people who were denied and rejected on their jobs. The Black Church

The Rev. Fred Shuttlesworth, the Rev. Ralph Abernathy, and Dr. Martin Luther King Jr. leading a march from Sixteenth Street Baptist Church toward downtown Birmingham on April 12, 1963

bestowed titles of leadership to people who were significantly unimportant in the larger community.

I developed a great love for the church through my maternal grand-mother, Willie Mae Sanford Cornelius, who was a Deaconess and the "Mother" of Mount Olive Baptist Church in Macon, Georgia. My grandmother displayed a unique commitment to that church and its programs. I was so impressed with her commitment that I followed her to worship services, revivals, mission meetings, and other experiences of the faithful, which afforded me the rich opportunity of really seeing what the Black Church is all about and its impact on the lives of people who commit themselves to it. While sitting in the pews surrounded by family and friends and listening to passionate messages of hope, I began to understand the significance of Jesus Christ and the prophetic and priestly role of the church in society.

My understanding of the prophetic ministry of the church and the poten-tial for liberation intensified when several pastors in Macon decided to protest racial discrimination in the mid-1960s. Our pastor, the Rev. E. S. Evans Sr., helped lead the effort to end segregated seating on public transportation.

Civil Rights demonstrators marching from the old St. James Missionary Baptist Church on Sixth Avenue North and Eleventh Street toward the downtown area of Birmingham

I remember hearing adults in my home talk about newspaper stories about the Reverend Evans and other pastors who led demonstrations and were arrested.

The commitment of the Reverend Evans to ministry and social change and the commitment of others living in Macon inspired me to attend Morehouse College in Atlanta, Georgia. While at Morehouse, I often heard the powerful sermons of Dr. Benjamin E. Mays, a minister and former president of the college. Morehouse College often invited prominent clergy such as Dr. Howard Thurman, Dr. Gayraud Wilmore, Dr. Otis Moss Jr., Dr. William Holmes Borders, and others to preach in Sale Hall Chapel and later Martin Luther King Jr. Memorial International Chapel. These prophetic voices were compelling witnesses of God's work in the world, and they led me to understand God's calling upon my life.

During my second semester at Morehouse I acknowledged a call to the ministry, and the pastor and congregation of Mount Olive Baptist Church affirmed my call. Accepting such a call meant that I would be completely dependent upon God for guidance and direction. It involved my willingness to go wherever I was sent and to become a servant of the people.

I saw this as an opportunity to fulfill an innate desire to help the black community, which was so paralyzed by systemic societal ills, including the critical issue of racism. Early in my studies at Morehouse I learned that the Black Church had resources that could be powerfully used both prophetically and priestly if they are harnessed properly. I came to understand that the role of the church must always focus on maintaining the message of the Liberator and preaching a gospel that liberates and frees all people.

After graduating from Morehouse, I enrolled in a Master of Divinity program at Colgate Rochester/Bexley Hall/Crozer Theological Seminary in Rochester, New York. I was impressed with Colgate's commitment to diversity and its historic emphasis on the social gospel and Black Church Studies. My experiences at Colgate deepened my understanding of the positive influence of the Black Church. Colgate was one of the first seminaries to develop a Black Church Studies Program, which offered all students an academic environment that fostered an appreciation for the significance of the Black Church and its liberating relevance to the universal Church of Christ.

While at Colgate I joined with other seminary students in working and volunteering in churches, soup kitchens, the Urban League, and other agencies. In that context what we studied in the classroom became practical and not just another exercise in biblical theory.

Upon graduating from seminary in 1984, I accepted the position of Minister of Youth and Education at Trinity Baptist Church in Pontiac, Michigan. For the next almost six years I worked under the Rev. Dr. Robert E. Bailey with a membership made of many professionals and blue collar workers in the automotive industry. Trinity remains the largest African American church in Oakland County, Michigan, and I believe my time of service there adequately prepared me for the stark realities of ministry.

When I learned about a vacancy at Sixteenth Street Baptist Church, I sent a letter to the pulpit committee, even though I had already concluded that they would be looking for someone with more experience than I had. Several weeks later I received a package of materials about the church, and I submitted my application. I prayed for God to direct my steps and the decision of the congregation, and others offered their prayers also.

The Rev. Dr. Christopher M. Hamlin in front of the Wales Window for Alabama at Sixteenth Street Baptist Church. Photograph by the Rev. Joseph Decatur.

Through the interview and search process I discovered that Sixteenth Street Baptist Church, one of the nation's most prestigious churches, was in spiritual ruin, paralyzed, in need of major renovation/restoration of its facilities, and sustained by less than 125 members. I also saw great potential and clearly heard God's call. On January 7, 1990, I became the sixteenth pastor of Sixteenth Street Baptist Church.

Behind the Stained Glass tells the 125-year story of this church, which I have come to love. Behind the stained glass of Sixteenth Street Baptist Church is a compelling story of hope and survival, of turmoil and transformation, and of revolution and reconciliation. Although there are many churches in the black community with unique histories, the story of Sixteenth Street Baptist Church stands as an example of a "love that forgives." Its story is similar to many congregations, yet it stands in a solitary reality unto itself. It is a powerful story of determination lived out in the lives of people and pastors who responded to God's voice in a "Magic City" that has often been filled with false promises and blatant lies. Behind the stained glass are people filled with a tenacious spirit determined to keep the doors of our church open and accessible to all people.

I hope that you, the reader, will come behind the stained glass and share in the lives of the people of Sixteenth Street Baptist Church. Parts of our story are wonderfully liberating. Other parts are scary, frightening, and will bring tears. Some parts tell of rejoicing and success, while others tell of divisive leadership squabbles and painful pastoral transitions. Part of our story is the most horrific event of America's Civil Rights Movement, the bombing that took the lives of four innocent children who were attending Sunday School on September 15, 1963.

Come behind the stained glass and you will see how the people of Sixteenth Street Baptist Church have changed, survived, and appropriated every aspect of their faith and history to make Birmingham a better place for all citizens.

Come behind the stained glass where nothing is hidden and where truth is echoed everywhere.

Christopher Maurice Hamlin
Birmingham, Alabama
1998

Behind the Stained Glass

A History of Sixteenth Street Baptist Church

Birmingham, Alabama, circa 1880

EARLY YEARS IN THE VALLEY

• • • • • •

When I arrived in Birmingham in 1990, I began studying the history of Sixteenth Street Baptist Church as well as the history of the City of Birmingham. The city's metropolitan population today is approximately 920,000 and the chief source of employment is fueled by the health profession, including hospitals (with the University of Alabama at Birmingham's University Hospital as the leader), clinics, research institutes, laboratories, and private practices. Colleges and universities; the construction, finance, insurance, and real estate industries; city, county, and regional governments; retail/wholesale trade; transportation and utilities; manufacturing and nonmanufacturing companies; and the service industry also support the city's economy. When I looked at Birmingham's development in the mid-1800s, however, I saw a different city and a vastly different social climate.

Birmingham developed in Jones Valley, a slight depression nestled below the mountains of central Alabama, and was chartered in December 1871 by Elyton Land Company (now Birmingham Realty) with 1,200 adventurous citizens. Since the land in Jefferson County around Birmingham was not fertile like that of the Black Belt region to the south, the growth of the city would never be dependent upon slaves cultivating crops. The emergence of Birmingham was the product of intersecting rail lines in the heart of the city planned by Elyton Land Company and the raw materials of iron, limestone, and coal, the necessary ingredients to produce steel. Birmingham was also the product of industrial giants, financial wizards, and land opportunists whose vision of what Jones Valley could become created a whirlwind of excitement. When the first steel was produced in Birmingham, the excitement heightened and caused the city to grow fast, so fast that it became known as the "Magic City."

The majority of the Magic City's early population came from three primary sources: poor whites and former slaves moving in from the country to find jobs and immigrants from Europe. The industrialists who spearheaded the development of Birmingham's steel industry came from outside the state, bringing with

3

them skills they learned in Europe and depending on the labor of others. As George R. Leighton stated in his article about Birmingham in the August 1937 issue of *Harper's Magazine*, "a group of speculators and industrialists in 1871 founded a city and peopled it with two races afraid of each other."

By 1890 blacks represented approximately 43 percent of Birmingham's population. The "magic" of the city demonstrated itself in constant growth and division along racial lines. Black men continued to do well by providing labor in the mines in and around Birmingham. The women worked as domestics for white families, and some of the men also worked menial jobs.

As Birmingham's black labor force increased and as racial discrimination through segregation intensified, the city's black citizens determined not to succumb to the evil forces of racism. With very few economic resources, blacks in Birmingham began to create the institutions they needed not only to survive, but to thrive. They created within the confines of segregation a self-contained community of businesses, services, churches, cultural amenities, and residential communities. These institutions were concentrated on Fourth Avenue North between Fourteenth and Eighteenth Streets. Because blacks were treated sorely by the white business community, it was important for them to be able to serve

Looking north on Twenty-first Street from Morris Avenue, circa 1890

4

themselves. "Blacks performed services that whites did not want to perform for blacks," explains J. Mason Davis, an attorney and businessman, in "The Other Side: The Story of Birmingham's Black Community," published by Birmingfind, a local history project.

In his 1988 booklet "Leadership Patterns in Birmingham's History, Auburn University historian Wayne Flynt characterized Birmingham as a city of paradoxes. Birmingham "claimed the South's highest ratio of immigrants, industrial workers, and blacks" but it "was surrounded by a white hinterland proud of its agrarian values, Anglo-Saxon population, and racial 'superiority.' A city which proclaimed itself a 'city of churches' selected for its municipal symbol a giant statue of the Roman god of metal-working (Vulcan) and the Roman goddess of the hearth (the Temple of Vesta)," wrote Flynt.

Elyton Land Company, which had founded Birmingham, donated land for a variety of uses. "The company's pro-growth policy of the early 1870s included giving lands to the railroads, industrial firms, the city and county (for parks, schools, and streets and alleys), and Christian denominations, both black and white," according to a newsletter published in February 1997 by the Birmingham Historical Society.

After the Civil War blacks and whites no longer worshiped together as the custom was during slavery, and by the end of Reconstruction black congregations had formed in most cities in the South. In *Reconstruction: America's Unfinished Revolution, 1863–1877* Eric Foner states that across the South "blacks emerging from slavery pooled their resources to purchase land and erect their own churches." He further states that during the Reconstruction period "religious convictions profoundly affected the way blacks understood the momentous events around them, the very language in which they expressed aspirations for justice and autonomy."

For blacks, the church was the one place where they could express their political convictions without fear of reprimand. Many blacks were attracted to the Baptist denomination because it was not controlled by bishops or any other hierarchical structure. They were free to develop their own worship and governing system. In *The Negro's Church*, their landmark book published in 1933, Benjamin E. Mays and Joseph W. Nicholson, confirmed that "the church was the first community or public organization that the Negro actually owned and completely controlled." They also suggested that even today "the Negro church is the most thoroughly owned and controlled public institution of the race."

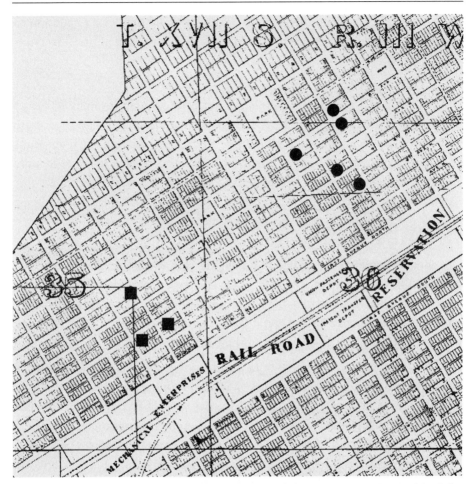

A portion of the Elyton Land Company Map showing the original land acquired and subdivided by that company, land forming today's city center, early 1870s. ● denotes sites donated to white Christian denominations (located near Capital Park, now Linn Park) and ■ denotes sites donated to black Christian denominations.

On April 20, 1873, in the heart of the City of Birmingham, in the midst of paradoxes and during a period of social change for blacks, the First Colored Baptist Church of Birmingham was born. Although Elyton Land Company donated land to both white and black religious groups, black congregations were not given land in the city center, and the first building used by the First Colored Baptist Church stood at Fourth Avenue North and Twelfth Street.

The September 1, 1873, deed for the First Colored Baptist Church records that James R. Powell, president of Elyton Land Company, received $1 from

Burton Hayes, John Redding, and Raphael Randall, the trustees of the church for the land for the building. White congregations could trade their land at a nominal cost for better sites, but black congregations "could not trade their land in if they wished to move from 'The Bottom,' an area along Thirteenth Street North near the industrial firms," reports the February 1997 newsletter of the Birmingham Historical Society. The deed for the First Colored Baptist Church stipulated that if the property ever changed from being used as a church it would revert to the Elyton Land Company.

The name assumed by the congregation reflects the time and racial climate of its birth. Unique to the South, many churches and other institutions of color were forced to make racial distinctions in their names or geographical locations. From its birth Birmingham had been divided geographically by race and class. Blacks lived either in company housing behind the houses of European immigrants and poor whites or west of the city center. The rich lived in the city center and south, and a strong Jewish community settled on Fifth Avenue North and later moved to the newly developed South Highlands area around Highland Avenue.

The First Colored Baptist Church of Birmingham organized in a small tinner's shop owned by a Mr. Paul on the corner of Fourth Avenue North and Twelfth Street. The Rev. James Readen and the Rev. Warner Reed are credited with organizing the church, with the Reverend Readen serving as pastor. The Reverend Readen resigned in 1876, and the Rev. A. C. Jackson became the church's second pastor. Although no historical records from this period have been preserved and no accurate accounts of the membership exist, the congregation evidently outgrew their small building under the leadership of the Reverend Jackson. The church moved into a building closer to the city center on Third Avenue North between Nineteenth and Twentieth Streets.

As the City of Birmingham continued to expand, the First Colored Baptist Church was requested to give up its land near the city center so retail stores could be built on it. Although there is no substantial information to make the case, a walk in this area of the city now would indicate the "city fathers" asked for the church's property as a way of removing a black religious presence on one of the city's major thoroughfares. If the First Colored Baptist Church of Birmingham had remained at this location, it would be in very close proximity to the prominent white flagship churches of Protestant denominations and the Roman Catholic Church. White churches seemed to have been placed in the vicinity of Capital Park (now Linn Park), while black churches were placed east and west of the park.

In July 1882 the congregation of the First Colored Baptist Church purchased from Elyton Land Company its current property at Sixth Avenue North and Sixteenth Street, at the northwest corner of West End Park (now Kelly Ingram Park), and changed its name to Sixteenth Street Baptist Church. (Even though the building faces Sixth Avenue North, a congregation organized in 1881 had its building on Sixth Avenue and Sixteenth Street South and had already assumed the name Sixth Avenue Baptist Church.)

The Reverend Jackson resigned in 1882, and in 1883 the congregation called the Rev. Dr. William Reuben Pettiford to be pastor of Sixteenth Street Baptist Church.

BUILDING A FIRM FOUNDATION

• • • • • •

The Rev. Dr. William Reuben Pettiford, a native of North Carolina, demonstrated great concern for the members of Sixteenth Street Baptist Church and the rest of the black community in Birmingham. It has been stated that he was a gifted preacher and people found it easy to follow his leadership. He organized the first missionary society in Birmingham.

During the ten years Dr. Pettiford served as the church's pastor, he displayed great business savvy. Under his leadership the congregation built a modern brick building with an impressive steeple. Many members mortgaged their homes so that Sixteenth Street Baptist Church could complete its building project on time. Undertaking and completing such a major construction project was quite an accomplishment for black people living

The Rev. Dr. William Reuben Pettiford, Pastor 1883–1893

in Birmingham in the late 1800s. Many white congregations in the city center had not completed their building projects, and the grand building completed by a black congregation must have created concern in the larger community. One can presuppose the prejudice that black people should not have been able to build such a facility when they did—especially not in Birmingham, Alabama!

The building was designed in the Gothic Revival style that typified church construction projects of the time. According to the National Park Service's 1993 Historic American Buildings Survey, "As typical of the style, variety of

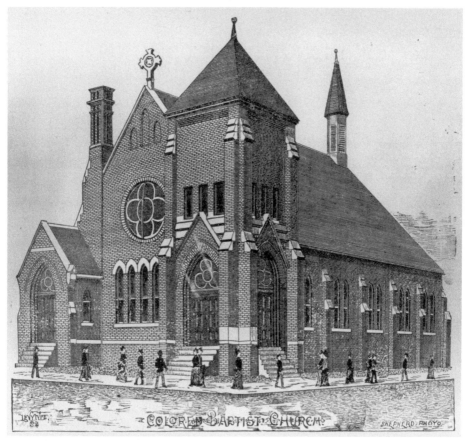

The first Sixteenth Street Baptist Church facility built on the current site, circa 1887

materials and irregularity in massing created a picturesque effect, with the entry and bell tower as the focal point, situated at the corner of Sixth Avenue and Sixteenth Street. Details included pointed-arched doorways and windows, steep buttresses, and a large quatrefoil window."

In his 1887 book *Jefferson County and Birmingham, Alabama: Historical and Biographical*, John Witherspoon DuBose gave this account:

> This is a brick edifice, erected on Sixteenth Street and Seventh [Sixth] Avenue, and an imposing style of ecclesiastical architecture. Rev. W. R. Pettiford is the pastor, and the church is in a highly prosperous condition. Mr. Pettiford has retained his charge since January 15, 1883, and under him the present beautiful church building has almost been completed. The history of the church building is one of honor to the pastor and his people.

10

With only $300 in the treasury they went on with laying the foundations, and step by step, with hard work and grievous delays, accomplished their purpose. The church has cost $6,000, and will, when fully completed, cost $8,500. The lot is worth about $10,000, or better.

With very few economic resources, blacks in Birmingham erected a facility for worship and religious education of significant size and sophistication before the city's whites did. The completion of the Sixteenth Street Baptist Church facility in 1884 demonstrates Dr. Pettiford's enormous leadership ability. His pastorate also elevated the church's standing in the Baptist work of the State of Alabama, and in 1887 Dr. Pettiford was elected president of the Alabama State Baptist Convention. He also served as president of the National Negro Business League and the National Negro Bankers Association.

Dr. Pettiford authored several books about religion and finances, and he worked closely with the black community in helping people acquire the "self-help" skills they needed to succeed. He also became involved in helping blacks in Birmingham better themselves financially. On October 15, 1890, he organized the Alabama Penny Savings Bank, the first black banking institution in Alabama. An article about the bank in volume XIV of the 1929 *Journal of Negro History* states, "The Bank, which was formed around a [nucleus] of black leaders, including B. H. Hudson Sr., N. B. Smith, Peter F. Clarke, A. H. Parker, J. O. Diaffay, and T. W. Walker, opened in the heart of the South."

According to program notes from a 1979 dedication ceremony for a historical marker in honor of Dr. Pettiford, people deposited more than $200,000 at the Alabama Penny Savings Bank's four locations—the main office in Birmingham and the branch offices in Montgomery, Anniston, and Selma. By 1907 it was the second largest black bank in the nation. "On October 11, 1911, the resources of the Alabama Penny Savings Bank were $421,596.51. A five-story reinforced-concrete bank building at 310 18th Street North was constructed. The Bank paid 4% interest on savings accounts. Shares in the Bank sold for $5.00 each."

Many black churches and more than a thousand homes were built by loans acquired through Alabama Penny Savings Bank before it closed on December 23, 1915, due to frozen assets from long-term loans, high withdrawals during the Christmas season, and its inability to acquire loans from a large white-owned

Alabama Penny Savings Bank, organized by the Rev. Dr. William Reuben Pettiford in 1890

bank in Birmingham. The twenty-five-year success of the bank is a credit to Dr. Pettiford and the men surrounding him.

Dr. Pettiford's interest in self-help also motivated him to be instrumental in creating the first black high school in Birmingham. Like others, Dr. Pettiford believed that education was the tool blacks needed to rise above Birmingham's segregation and discrimination. According to *The Other Side: The Story of Birmingham's Black Community*:

> In the early years of the Birmingham black community, educational concerns centered less on professional degrees than on establishing grammar schools. The first black public grammar school in Birmingham was Lane School, founded in 1886 on the Southside. Carrie A. Tuggle built Tuggle Institute, a popular private school and orphanage on Enon Ridge, in 1903.
>
> There was no black high school in Jefferson County before 1900. Parents who wanted to educate their children beyond grammar school sent them to Tuskegee Institute or Talladega College, which had high schools at the time. In 1899, however, a group of blacks led by William R. Pettiford requested that the city establish a public high school for blacks.

In 1900 the Birmingham Board of Education appointed Arthur H. Parker the first principal of the new school, Industrial High School (later renamed A. H. Parker High School). Parker, one of Dr. Pettiford's business associates at Alabama Penny Savings Bank, followed the educational philosophy of Booker T. Washington and was a firm advocate of industrial education. Even though Parker espoused this philosophy, many of Industrial High School's students received a liberal arts education provided by Parker and the faculty of the school.

In 1893 Dr. Pettiford resigned from the pastorate of Sixteenth Street to devote more time to Alabama Penny Savings Bank, and the congregation called the Rev. Dr. T. L. Jordan, of Mississippi, to be their pastor. The Reverend Jordan reportedly was an eloquent preacher and a great debater, but his five years as pastor were not highlighted by major events in the life of the congregation.

When Dr. Jordan resigned in 1898 to return to his native state, the congregation called the Rev. Dr. Charles L. Fisher to be their pastor. Dr. Fisher, who served from September 1898 until 1911, would later gain the distinct honor of being the only pastor to serve two pastoral administrations at Sixteenth Street Baptist Church, his second term beginning in 1921 and lasting until 1930.

Shortly after Dr. Fisher arrived in Birmingham from Eutaw, Alabama, the congregation of Sixteenth Street Baptist Church experienced a

The Rev. Dr. T. L. Jordan,
Pastor 1893–1898

The Rev. Dr. Charles L. Fisher,
Pastor 1898–1911 and 1921–1930

Architect Wallace A. Rayfield

major setback. According to church records, it was determined in 1900 that the twenty-five-year-old building needed major repairs totaling $2,000 and the congregation decided that it was more prudent to build a new building than continuing to invest in the old one. In 1909, before the congregation had raised $1,000 toward building a new facility, the City of Birmingham condemned the existing building and barred the congregation from using it.

The city ordered the congregation of Sixteenth Street Baptist Church to raze its facility. Although church historians have not been able to determine whether the building did indeed have any structural problems, it seems unlikely that a brick building built less than thirty years earlier would have been structurally unsound.

In the early 1900s blacks remained a minority in Birmingham's population of 38,415. Blacks were not represented in Birmingham's government, and some decisions made by the city commission, including this one, appear to have been used to tarnish and impede progress in the black community. Despite this harsh, unfair treatment, blacks continued to excel and improve life for themselves and their families.

The congregation had no choice but to comply with the city's order to raze their building—but they determined to remain a viable worshiping community in downtown Birmingham. They commissioned black architect Wallace A. Rayfield, who had relocated to Birmingham after teaching at Tuskegee Institute, to design a their new facility.

In his booklet "W. A. Rayfield: Pioneer Black Architect of Birmingham, Ala.," the late historian Dr. Charles A. Brown, a Deacon of Sixteenth Street Baptist Church, said that Rayfield was Birmingham's first black architect. Born in Macon, Georgia, on May 11, 1874, Rayfield was taken at age 12 to Washington, D.C., to live with an aunt after the passing of his mother. After graduating from high school, Rayfield entered Howard University and later continued his studies at Pratt Institute—Columbia University in Brooklyn,

New York. He graduated in 1899 with a certificate in architecture and accepted a position with A. B. Mullett and Company Architects in Washington, D.C.

At the invitation of Booker T. Washington, Rayfield taught at Tuskegee Institute for eight years. He moved to Birmingham in 1907 and established the first black architectural business in the state. It was only natural that the bulk of Rayfield's work would be found in black churches. He is credited with designing not only Sixteenth Street Baptist Church but also Sixth Avenue Baptist Church (its former building), South Elyton Baptist, First Congregational Church (its former building), St. Luke A.M.E Church, and 32nd Street Baptist Church. In 1909 A.M.E. Zion Church selected Rayfield to design all its buildings, including churches, parsonages, and educational facilities. A recent discovery of Rayfield's advertisement plates in a barn in Bessemer, Alabama, demonstrates the caliber of the architect's work and the scope of his range beyond Birmingham and Alabama. Rayfield also briefly taught at Industrial (now A. H. Parker) High School.

In 1909 Sixteenth Street Baptist Church's leadership rejected Rayfield's first design but accepted his second design, which was unparalleled to anything previously designed by a black man in the City of Birmingham. Thomas

Under the leadership of the Rev. Dr. Charles L. Fisher (inset), the congregation of Sixteenth Street Baptist Church rejected architect Wallace A. Rayfield's first design for their new facility.

15

Cornelius Windham, who was a member and Trustee of the congregation as well as a builder, took Rayfield's design and built the facility that the congregation of Sixteenth Street Baptist Church continues to use today.

Windham had established Windham Brothers Construction Company in Arkansas in 1895 and came to Birmingham in the early 1900s. He and his family joined Sixteenth Street Baptist Church, and he was elected to the Board of Trustees and served as its chairman. In "Contractor & Sportin' Man," an article that ran in the February 22, 1992, edition of *The Birmingham News*, Larry Ragan said that when Windham arrived in Birmingham "many of the city's prominent black professional and white-collar workers lived in Smithfield, a community just to the west of the Birmingham city center." Ragan noted that Windham "bought a block of real estate in Smithfield and built a two-story brick mansion that reflected not only his wealth, but also his business abilities." Windham Brothers Construction Company became the principal company to build homes of prominent black people in Birmingham.

The congregation signed the contract with Windham on March 8, 1909, and work immediately began on the new building. With the Sixteenth Street Baptist Church facility being one of the shining examples of their work nearly completed in 1911, Rayfield and Windham established themselves as Birmingham's premiere church architects and builders.

Rayfield and Windham partnered in designing and building many homes in the Smithfield area of the city. These homes show the depth of the abilities of these two extraordinary men and their commitment to the black community. Together these men also designed and built the Masonic and Pythian Temples in the heart of the black business district.

The Great Depression, however, adversely affected Rayfield's business and shortened his life. According to Dr. Brown's booklet, Rayfield's "long and distinguished career terminated

Thomas Cornelius Windham, founder of Windham Brothers Construction Company

16

with declining health and fortune." Rayfield passed on February 28, 1941, and was buried in Greenwood (Woodlawn) Cemetery.

Windham Brothers Construction Company continued to operate until 1966, when Lewis Sandy Windham, the only son of Thomas, passed. Like his father, Lewis had served as a Trustee of Sixteenth Street Baptist Church.

The Sixteenth Street Baptist Church facility cost nearly $35,000 to build. The building's modified Romanesque and Byzantine architectural design features twin towers with pointed domes, a cupola over the sanctuary accessible by a wide stairway, and a large basement auditorium with several rooms along the east and west sides. This grand new home gave testimony to the congregation's spirit of determination.

When it was dedicated in 1911, the Sixteenth Street Baptist Church building was the largest in the black community. According to the National Park Service's 1993 Historic American Buildings Survey, "The prominence of the structure—a reflection of the prominence of its congregation—coupled with its size and downtown location made Sixteenth Street Baptist Church a focal point for various activities in the black community." At the time it was the "only large centrally located black-owned edifice in the city."

With the completion of the building, Sixteenth Street Baptist Church's role in the community expanded to a new level. The residential and business black community that surrounded the facility found it to be a warm, inviting environment for many community events. With a seating capacity of 1,600, the building often served as a concert hall, featuring the Fisk Jubilee Singers, quartets, and other music groups, as well as providing a convenient site for many other community-wide activities.

John Hope of Morehouse College, Mary McLeod Bethune of Bethune–Cookman College, Adam Clayton Powell, and many others frequently visited the church's pulpit. According to the National Park Service's 1993 Historic American Buildings Survey, "Politics, both local and national, were debated at Sixteenth Street, including National Association for the Advancement of Colored People (NAACP) meetings—one to discuss paying poll tax and another upon the return of the delegation to the Republican National Convention—were held, as was a meeting of the suffrage league." After many years of opening its doors for cultural and civic events, Sixteenth Street Baptist Church became known as "Everybody's Church," a name that continues to be ascribed to the facility today.

Sixteenth Street Baptist Church, designed by architect Wallace A. Rayfield and built by Windham Brothers Construction Company, 1909–1911. Photograph by Jet Lowe from the National Park Service's 1993 Historic American Buildings Survey.

The sanctuary of Sixteenth Street Baptist Church before the February 16, 1923, fire. As part of the renovations made after the fire, the organ and choir loft were lowered to their current positions.

Under Dr. Fisher's pastorate the congregation grew from 420 to 1,350. This increase in membership corresponded to the city's growing black labor pool and the influence of professional blacks. From 1900 to 1910, Birmingham's population increased 245.4 percent.

Seeing his task of building a new facility completed, Dr. Fisher resigned as pastor of Sixteenth Street Baptist Church in 1911, and the congregation called the Rev. Dr. J. A. Whitted of Winston–Salem, North Carolina. The Reverend Whitted enhanced the new facility by installing a two-manual Pilcher Pipe Organ in 1912, the first pipe organ in a black religious facility in Birmingham. The inclusion of this powerful instrument in the new building established the high caliber of worship services held at Sixteenth Street Baptist Church.

Mr. Bill Pilcher, of Pilcher Organ Company, built the two-manual organ in Louisville, Kentucky, and had it transported to Birmingham. The instrument, which included thirteen ranks of pipes, cost $2,100. Pilcher built 1,941 organs before the company went out of business in 1945.

The congregation also furnished the sanctuary during Dr. Whitted's five-year pastorate. When Dr. Whitted resigned in 1916, the church's debt stood at $31,000.

The Rev. Dr. A. C. Williams of Los Angeles, California, became the pastor of Sixteenth Street Baptist Church in June 1916. Williams was a graduate of Morehouse College, and his training matched the educational attainment of the congregation. Church records reveal that Williams was well known for singing, and he often gave concerts in the church and throughout the community to enthusiastic listeners. His wife, who was a capable organist, often accompanied him.

Dr. Williams, who was particularly interested in youth, organized a youth department to increase the membership of the church. He also organized the Pastor's Aid Club, Willing Workers, and the Sixteenth Street Baptist Church Orchestra.

Under the leadership of Dr. Williams, the ministry of Sixteenth Street Baptist Church continued to grow. The church's increase in membership reflected the population growth of the City of Birmingham, which by 1920 had increased by 34.8 percent over the previous ten years to total 178,806.

The Rev. Dr. J. A. Whitted,
Pastor 1911–1916

The Rev. Dr. A. C. Williams,
Pastor 1916–1920

Dr. Williams left the pastorate of Sixteenth Street Baptist Church in 1920 to work in Detroit, Michigan. Dr. Williams's and Dr. Whitted's pastorates had left the church with an indebtedness of more than $25,000.

With their strong desire to eliminate the debt, the congregation requested that the Rev. Dr. Charles L. Fisher consider returning as pastor. In a letter signed by the secretary of the church and chairman of the Board of Deacons and dated January 14, 1921, the congregation conveyed their selection of Dr. Fisher as "permanent pastor" of the church.

Dear sir & brother:

This comes to inform you that at our recent church conference Tuesday night Jan. 11th. you were elected permanent Pastor of Sixteenth Street Baptist Church.

This action was taken by the church after months and weeks of research and investigation and a week of prayer. A month's notice had been given in advance and the announcement given at each service calling the membership's attention to the fact that such action would be taken.

This call not only expresses the wishes of the vast majority of the adult members of the church but is an answer to the prayers of the ministry and laity of all denominations through out our city, district and the State of Alabama.

In extending this call we feel that you are the one man that can redeem the church and restore it to its rightful place in the conduct of the program of social, moral, and religious uplift of our community and state. Your failure to accept this call would be as dire a calamity as the [siege] of confusion through which we pass. We therefore urge and pray that you accept the call and arrange to come to us at the earliest date. We feel thoroughly convinced that the call is of God.

Yours in His name.

On February 16, 1921, Dr. Fisher wrote to say that he had submitted his resignation to Union Baptist Church of Hartford, Connecticut, and regrettably it had been accepted. "Now that my resignation has been presented to the church, although it was indefinitely postponed by a unanimous vote, I feel at

The Senior Choir of Sixteenth Street Baptist Church, circa 1917

liberty to accept formally your call extended to me January 11, 1921, to become your permanent pastor," wrote Dr. Fisher.

Dr. Fisher's immediate task when he returned to Sixteenth Street Baptist Church was to help reduce the sizable debt of $28,000. The congregation received substantial help in this effort through a damaging fire on February 16, 1923. Although church records do not go into great detail, they suggest that the fire started in the area where coal for heating was stored. The congregation was adequately compensated through an insurance company that paid a claim after the fire.

Using the insurance money and approximately $11,000 raised through Dr. Fisher's initiatives, the congregation had major modifications made to the sanctuary while the church was being repaired. The choir loft and organ were lowered from their original position above the pulpit area to their present position. The organ pipes and chamber were also lowered to their current position. Other modifications also made at this time enhanced the quality of worship services and other uses of the facility.

It is obvious that these changes in the facility and the fervor that Dr. Fisher brought to the ministry of Sixteenth Street Baptist Church had a positive effect on the congregation. In 1923 the membership experienced substantial growth, with approximately 228 persons received as candidates for baptism, 70 by restoration, and 438 by Christian experience. By 1927 the "Communion Roll" of the church listed 923 members.

Conference minutes report several congregational actions taken during Dr. Fisher's pastorate to enforce certain church discipline. The congregation placed members who missed three consecutive communions on inactive status until the congregation restored them to the "Communion Roll."

When three women who were members of Sixteenth Street Baptist Church were rebaptized at a pentecostal church in "Jesus' name only," an action deemed doctrinally improper, they were brought before the congregation to renounce the second baptism. The women were given ample opportunity to apologize to the congregation, but they failed to acknowledge their error and were removed from the membership of the church. Although the three women protested the congregation's decision, it stood, and they never returned to Sixteenth Street Baptist Church.

Dr. Fisher recognized the importance of keeping members informed about church affairs, and he started two weekly publications, *The Churchman* and *The Evangel*. Both of these widely circulated newsletters reported information about the church, denominational efforts, and community events. The newsletters were sponsored by paid advertisements from both the black and white business communities. Dr. Fisher also occasionally published sermons in the *Birmingham Reporter*, including "Slander," which appeared in the December 18, 1926, issue.

Dr. Fisher resigned from the pastorate of Sixteenth Street Baptist Church in September 1930. In his letter of resignation dated September 28, he wrote:

Considering the fact that we had a heart to heart talk as pastor and church on last Sunday concerning the affairs of the Church, I do not deem it necessary to set forth more reasons in this communication as to the advisability of accepting a position of which you are in full knowledge.

The Evangel

"And I if I be lifted up from the earth will draw all men unto me." John 12:32.

PUBLISHED BY SIXTEENTH STREET BAPTIST CHURCH
Fostered by the Brotherhood

VOL. 1   BIRMINGHAM, ALA., MAY 11, 1928   NO. 5

CHURCH ROSTER

Dr. C. L. Fisher, A. M., D. D., Pastor
Mrs. M. L. M. Hooks, Clerk
Mr. P. F. Clarke, Treasurer

TRUSTEE BOARD
Mr. T. C. Windham, Chairman

DEACON BOARD
Mr. W. T. Clark, Chairman

DEACONESS BOARD
Mrs. Ella C. Harris, Chairman

SENIOR CHOIR
Mrs. M. L. Parrish, President
Miss Mabel Barker, Organist
Mr. D. D. Mitchell, Chorister

JUNIOR CHOIR
Miss Alton Taylor, President
Miss Mary A. Clarke, Pianist
Mr. D. D. Mitchell, Chorister
Mr. A. F. Smart, Jr., Orchestra Leader

SUNDAY SCHOOL
Mr. J. C. L. Curry, Superintendent

SENIOR B. Y. P. U.
Mr. J. L. Perry, President

JUNIOR B. Y. P. U.
Rosetta Clarke, President

MISSIONARY SOCIETY
Mrs. L. D. Cobb, President

USHER BOARD
Mr. R. W. Ashe, President

LAYMAN'S MOVEMENT
Mr. J. H. Bunn, Sr., President

BOOSTING

The coming of the Jones Valley Boosters' Club to our Church Sunday night, April 29th, suggested this topic to me. This club of men headed by Mr. Rasberry as President and Mr. W. B, Driver as chairman of the Executive Committee, rings true to its name. They are a jolly set of boosters. They do not censioriously criticise **anybody.** But they spend their time gladly in pushing, not knocking, the other fellow, and helping him, if he will only try, to climb the hill of difficulty. We had only to call up these officers and extend them an informal invitation to visit at the time above named, and render us a program.

They readily accepted. We got more than we asked. They brought with them several delegates to the National Council of Boys Clubs: among whom were the National President and the National Secretary, and several others, both men and women, white and black. They DID give us a splendid program as we requested, using principally the delegates to the Council; but they did more. They raised $110.00 as a contribution to our Mortgage fund. NOW THAT IS BOOSTING. We are hereby expressing on behalf of our congregation, our appreciation and gratitude. You have a standing invitation to come to us on short notice..

Brother, what are you; a booster or a knocker? Do you say everything good you can for your neighbor, your business associates, your social pals, your fraternal organizations, your church? Do you do everything you can when needed to help them? If you do, then you are a booster. If you do NOT, then you are a knocker. You need not speak any words, or take any active steps against them. If you do not help when needed, though you are able to do so, you are a knocker. WHAT SIDE ARE YOU ON? —THE PASTOR.

MISSIONARY SOCIETY

The Missionary Society held a very interesting session at its monthly meeting Monday the 7th. There were six circles present, reporting excellent work done.

Circle No. 3b with Mrs. Fannie Curry as Leader, is the last Circle organized under the new plan, it is not quite a month old, but took the banner, making a report of money raised $27.00. Much credit is due these few faithful workers for their zeal. The Society as a whole decided to to be represented in the Mortgage Burning Rally as one soldier, giving $15.00. The President, Mrs. L. D. Cobb, made an earnest appeal that the women would become more conscientious about the great work to be accomplished through the channels of the Missionary Society. Attention is now turned to the coming session of the State Convention to be held in June.

NOTES

Mr. Edward Hutchinson, the son of Mr. and Mrs. J. E. Hutchinson, 1410 College Street who is a Sophomore at Meharry, will work in New York during vacation this Summer.

Mr. A. Franklin Fisher, son of Dr. and Mrs. C. L. Fisher was the winner of the first prize in the National Negro Oratorical Contest held in Charleston, W. Va., May 4th.

VISITORS ARE ALWAYS WELCOME.

The Rev. Dr. C. L. Fisher and his family

Therefore, I am hereby tendering my resignation as pastor of Sixteenth Street Baptist Church to accept the position of Head Professor in the Theological Department of Selma University; to take effect October 28, 1930.

The congregation responded to this letter of resignation with a resolution acknowledging their appreciation and highest esteem for Dr. Fisher and his years of ministry, during which 514 members joined Sixteenth Street Baptist Church. The congregation extended their sincere blessings upon him.

BUILDING THE WALLS

• • • • • •

By the time Dr. Fisher resigned from his second pastorate at Sixteenth Street Baptist Church in 1930, Birmingham's population had grown by more than 45 percent to a total of 259,678. The church's importance and presence in the community had grown with the city's population, and the congregation continued its longtime practice of allowing outside groups to use its facilities for various meetings and social events.

The minutes from congregational conferences held in the early thirties indicate the beginning of financial difficulties for the congregation of Sixteenth Street Baptist Church, even though under Dr. Fisher's leadership they had reduced their debt by 90 percent. Conference minutes show that the congregation voted to cut the salaries of the church's staff two times, the "Current Expense" (the general operating budget of the church) reflected a deficit of $535.80, and several bills remained outstanding.

The minutes also reflect open hostility from some members of the congregation about the way the lay leadership was "running" the business affairs of the church. Accusations made by one church member against another inflamed several meetings.

Sixteenth Street Baptist Church obviously needed strong pastoral leadership, but the congregation seemed to be struggling to identify someone to call as pastor. After Dr. Fisher's resignation, the church employed several ministers to preach, including some who were viewed as potential pastors.

The Rev. Benjamin A. Hawkins, former pastor of St. Joseph Baptist Church, served as interim pastor of Sixteenth Street Baptist Church during this time and did a commendable job of keeping the membership focused. The Reverend Hawkins worked full time as the death-claim adjuster for Atlanta Life Insurance Company and did not desire to become pastor of the church. As interim pastor, however, he provided valuable service as a reconciler between divisive factions of the congregation.

The Rev. Benjamin A. Hawkins, Interim Pastor

Other ministers also moderated congregational conferences and served as supply preachers during this interim period. Some of these ministers played a significant role in helping keep the congregation together, while others only added to the congregation's confusion. The Reverend Hawkins stands alone as the minister who helped Sixteenth Street Baptist Church the most during this and several other times of crisis.

During the early thirties the congregation of Sixteenth Street Baptist Church began a pattern of being unable to develop a successful process for selecting pastors. The congregation seemed to grow impatient with the first pulpit committee convened after Dr. Fisher's resignation in 1930. At a congregational conference one of the church members made a motion to disband the committee because of its apparent inability to complete its task, another member seconded the motion, and the congregation quickly passed it.

Sometimes when a pulpit committee presented a minister's name to the congregation, the church members would vote to remove that minister from consideration. The Rev. A. Wendell Ross of Canton, Ohio, found much displeasure with Sixteenth Street Baptist Church's process. After the pulpit committee presented his name to the congregation, several church members meticulously scrutinized his character. In a pattern that is reported repeatedly in the minutes of congregational conferences, the Reverend Ross came to Birmingham to defend his reputation. At the conclusion of a meeting between the Reverend Ross and the Official Board (the church's Deacons and Trustees), the Reverend Ross returned to Ohio without receiving a call to become the church's pastor.

Cautioning the members of Sixteenth Street Baptist Church to do the right thing, Trustee Thomas Cornelius Windham made a powerful statement at the October 7, 1931, congregational conference.

The church is not a political body in which canvassing and similar practices must be used to direct the work. This is not a time for differences and divisions. Do not let the public know of your disagreements. Fifty, sixty, or even seventy percent of the membership is not sufficient to call a pastor. No minister would like to come into a divided church.

Windham's statement expressed concern about the divisive factions within the church as well as about the public's perception of what the church's leadership was doing. The congregation of Sixteenth Street Baptist Church considered itself to be the premiere black church of Birmingham, and Windham and other leaders did not want the public to know that the October 7th meeting had ended in much confusion.

Once again the Reverend Hawkins stepped in to help the congregation focus on what they ought to be doing to move forward toward calling a pastor. He urged the congregation to put aside any strife and contentions that would disrupt the harmony they needed and pleaded for members to earnestly possess the spirit of Christ.

The December 9, 1931, conference minutes record a membership of 680, a significant drop from the almost 1,000 members under Dr. Fisher's leadership. At the end of 1931, as they did every year, the congregation elected new leaders to serve the coming year for the different church auxiliaries, including the Sunday School, Baptist Young People's Union (BYPU), Young Ladies Usher Board, Deaconess Board, Senior Choir, Missionary Society, Deacons, and Trustees.

At the December 20, 1931, congregational conference, a letter from the Rev. Dr. S. A. Owen, of the historic Metropolitan Baptist Church in Memphis, was read. Dr. Owen stated that he had resigned from Metropolitan Baptist Church with the intention of "casting his lot with the members and friends" of Sixteenth Street Baptist Church. He also stated that he "would pay the church a visit December 27th."

After meeting Dr. Owen and his wife on December 27, 1931, the congregation called him to be their pastor. Dr. Owen accepted but stated that he would not be able to begin serving full-time for at least ninety days. He asked that the Reverend Hawkins continue to serve as interim pastor.

Dr. Owen's tenure as pastor received early warning signs of hostility. One time when he was moderating a church conference, three members openly questioned his salary, which had been voted on at a previous conference. Ella Harris, an active and devoted church member, stated that it was pitiful "to see how they were still trying to keep up confusion in the church just to carry out their own selfish aims." In concluding the meeting Dr. Owen stated his displeasure at what had been said. He admonished the congregation not to talk too much and told them bluntly that it is not always good to say everything one is thinking.

In a special called meeting on April 4, 1932, Dr. Owen informed the congregation that he was ill and required rest in order to fully recover from the "flu." The congregation voted unanimously to grant him a leave of absence.

Reportedly one member of the church anonymously sent letters to Dr. and Mrs. Owen. Although church records do not give detailed information about the content of the letters, the decision by the congregation to condemn such letter-writing infers that the letters were highly negative.

The Rev. Dr. David F. Thompson, Pastor 1932–1943

On June 15, 1932, the congregation accepted a letter of resignation from Dr. Owen. His letter is not included in the church's records, and the conference minutes give no indication of why he resigned. Furthermore, Dr. Owen's name has never appeared in the official listing of pastors of Sixteenth Street Baptist Church.

For the second time in less than two years, the congregation found itself without a full-time pastor. In May 1932, the month before Dr. Owen resigned, the Rev. Dr. David F. Thompson, pastor of Tabernacle Baptist Church in Augusta, Georgia, had come to Sixteenth Street Baptist Church to conduct revival services. His time at the church had received very positive comments, and he had left an indelible favorable impression on the membership.

When Dr. Owen resigned, the congregation extended a call to Dr. Thompson to become their new pastor. Dr. Thompson accepted and moved with his family into the church's parsonage on November 16, 1932. He assumed full responsibility for Sixteenth Street Baptist Church on November 20th.

Dr. Thompson's pastorate coincided with another major surge of growth in Birmingham's population, and the church's membership increased accordingly. Church records reveal that membership totaled 714 in 1932.

Dr. Thompson also increased Sixteenth Street Baptist Church's visibility in local, state, and national religious work. A graduate of Virginia Union University, Dr. Thompson recognized the value of education, and he enhanced the church's Christian education program. During his pastorate, the church held its first Vacation Bible School, with Myrtle Clarke providing the leadership. Members of the congregation wrote and published the Vacation Bible School materials, and young people from the metropolitan community attended. Also during Dr. Thompson's pastorate, Boy Scout Troop No. 131 was organized at the church, with P. D. Jackson serving as Scoutmaster and Felix Paul as his assistant.

The congregation purchased copies of the *Broadman Hymnal* to use during worship services, and the choirs and an orchestra performed cantatas at Christmas and Easter. Notable musicians, including Josephine Harreld, a talented pianist, presented concerts. Other cultural and community events continued to highlight the important role Sixteenth Street Baptist Church played in Birmingham.

Throughout his eleven-year tenure, Dr. Thompson focused on reducing the church's indebtedness and developing a systematic approach to budgeting. He implemented the pledge system and asked the members to submit financial pledges for the next year's church budget. The congregation also held several special rally days to liquidate outstanding bills.

Before implementing the pledge system, the congregation borrowed money to liquidate the church's debt. The congregation also asked the staff to take a reduction in pay so the church could save approximately $250.00. Monthly congregational conferences allowed careful scrutiny of the church's finances and enhanced the dissemination of this information. The conferences also became opportunities for some members to display venomous behavior that was often called into question by other members.

The B. F. Anderson Bible Class, June 4, 1939. The Rev. Dr. David F. Thompson is the third person from the left on the front row.

The crowning moment of Dr. Thompson's ministry came on October 20, 1940, when the congregation paid off the mortgage held by the estate of T. C. Windham. The congregation had approved raising the $4,700 mortgage through sacrificial gifts. The Deacons pledged $500, the Trustees pledged $700, and the congregation assumed the balance of $3,500. The estate of Mr. Windham helped by reducing the final mortgage by $947.96. The success of this financial campaign led to a public worship service called "The Mortgage Burning."

Dr. Thompson, like Dr. Owen before him, experienced the brutality of letters circulated throughout the congregation questioning his morals. In a letter dated June 25, 1941, the officers of the church responded to complaints stated in a June 9th letter they had received from several brothers. The substance of the complaints were immoral conduct, renting quarters in the parsonage, neglecting the pulpit, and having a bad temper.

An investigative committee of the Deacon Board found no proof of immoral conduct, but Dr. Thompson did admit to renting out a bedroom in the parsonage, preaching at services at various funeral homes for persons who were unchurched, conducting revivals for other churches, and possessing a "bad temper." Seventy-eight of the church members attending the conference when the charges were discussed accepted Dr. Thompson's statement of "wrongdoing"; one member voted not to accept it. Although the congregation did not levy disciplinary actions against Dr. Thompson, he felt the sting of those members who sought ways of ending his career at Sixteenth Street Baptist Church.

Dr. Thompson's pastorate came to an unexpected end February 25, 1943, when he suddenly fell ill. He did not recover from his illness, and the congregation of Sixteenth Street Baptist Church mourned his passing with Mrs. Thompson and the couple's five children at the funeral rites held in Birmingham. Officers and members of the church accompanied the family to the final obsequies for Dr. Thompson held in Columbia, South Carolina.

Dr. Thompson's legacy as pastor of Sixteenth Street Baptist Church remains strong among members who were here during his tenure. They remember that he encouraged them to make the ministry of their church successful. They also remember the many challenges they faced in trying to keep financially solvent and how Dr. Thompson's sheer determination and leadership kept their church afloat.

On the recommendation of the Official Board given at a conference on September 8, 1943, the congregation voted to extend a call to the Rev. Dr. D. Albert Jackson to become the pastor of Sixteenth Street Baptist Church. Several church members attending that meeting spoke glowingly of Dr. Jackson's abilities and gifts. At the time Dr. Jackson was serving as pastor of Mount Zion Baptist Church in Knoxville, Tennessee, and the Pulpit Committee sent representatives once to Knoxville and also once to Nashville to interview Dr. Jackson and others. The minutes of the conference reflect the sentiment that the trips to Knoxville and Nashville had been necessary because the committee did not want any surprises or issues of morality to hinder its recommendation.

On October 10, 1943, Dr. Jackson, his wife, and their son came to worship at Sixteenth Street Baptist Church. During his visit Dr. Jackson was asked when could he assume the pastorate of the church, and his response

Sunday morning worship service, circa 1940

was not a firm one, which seemed to irritate some of the members. Dr. Jackson stated that he needed to pray about the situation and wait for God's direction. He encouraged the congregation to develop a vision for their future ministries, and he spoke against cliques being formed and meetings that were taking place in various homes.

As with other ministers who had been considered for the pastorate of Sixteenth Street Baptist Church, Dr. Jackson acknowledged receiving letters from members of the congregation. He also acknowledged that he was not pleased with the tactics that the Pulpit Committee members who visited Knoxville had used in securing information about him, and he spoke vehemently about one of the church representatives staying at the home of a Methodist family—"a rival," as he put it.

In a special called conference on January 11, 1944, the congregation was read a letter from Dr. Jackson stating that he would not accept the call to become the church's pastor. Several members expressed outrage for waiting for a response from Dr. Jackson when it was obvious that he was not interested in Sixteenth Street Baptist Church. Other members criticized the Deacons for usurping their authority in acting without the church's permission in sending committee members to Knoxville and Nashville. The pattern of infighting between various members over the process being used to find a new pastor continued to be repeated.

After much debate, the congregation charged the Deacons to present a recommendation for a pastor by January 21, 1944. Once again the congregation called upon the Rev. Benjamin A. Hawkins to serve as interim pastor, and once again he urged the congregation to stay focused on its mission and the ministry of Sixteenth Street Baptist Church.

At a special called conference on January 21, 1944, the congregation voted to extend a call to the Rev. Dr. A. B. Coleman, pastor of Shiloh Baptist Church of Jacksonville, Florida. During the meeting letters from Dr. D. V. Jemison, president of the National Baptist Convention, Mrs. D. F. Thompson, and Dr. A. M. Townsend, of the Convention's Publishing Board, were read as testimonials to Reverend Coleman's qualifications.

Dr. Coleman visited Sixteenth Street Baptist Church for the first time on February 15, 1944. As part of his visit he requested a meeting with the church's auxiliary leaders and outlined his ideas for expanding the ministry of the church

A Sixteenth Street Baptist Church Sunday School class, circa 1940. The Rev. Dr. David F. Thompson is the last person on the righthand side of the front row.

to be more responsive to the needs of the members and potential members. Dr. Coleman also suggested that the congregation finance the ministry through tithing. All of the leaders of the church's auxiliaries agreed with Dr. Coleman's suggestions and pledged to support him.

On February 17, 1944, Dr. Coleman met with a group of young people at the church. He wanted to introduce himself to them and also begin the process of making them more involved in the life of the congregation. He stressed that young people spent a lot of time in secular education and little time in religious activities. His goal was that Sixteenth Street Baptist Church would be instrumental in providing more activities for young people, and he suggested creating booster clubs for two age groups. These two clubs would offer opportunities for young people to participate in the church at a level that would be exciting for them. Sixteenth Street Baptist Church did not have a large population of young people at that time, and Dr. Coleman saw that as a critical issue.

Several members expressed the need for an education building to facilitate the plans that Dr. Coleman had presented. Although Dr. Coleman did not reject this idea, he stressed that church growth should take priority over the need for an educational building.

At various turns in Sixteenth Street Baptist Church's history, the congregation compared itself to the congregations of other churches in the community. The congregation did not want Sixteenth Street Baptist Church to be viewed as doing less than any other church. Other Birmingham congregations provided basic amenities for the pastor and his family, and certain members of Sixteenth Street Baptist Church expressed the concern that the community might perceive that they were not taking care of their pastor.

During a congregational conference on June 14, 1944, church members spent considerable energies discussing the need for a parsonage for Dr. Coleman and his family. Since the parsonage next door to the sanctuary building had been converted into educational space, the congregation selected a house to accommodate Dr. Coleman and his family. The house cost $5,250 and needed approximately $2,000 in repairs and furnishings.

Several members of the congregation expressed concern that the church not expand beyond its means and ability to manage a new property. Other members stressed that Dr. Coleman had presented a program to the church that was forward looking, and they believed it was proper and appropriate to provide this home for their pastor and his family.

The chairman of the Deacon Board, P. D. Davis, stated that he wanted everyone to "toe the mark. Other churches are doing big things while we are arguing and making points of order," he said. The congregation's decision to provide a parsonage for the pastor resulted in a major discussion during which many members expressed their ill feelings about the matter.

On July 2, 1944, the congregation received a letter from Dr. Coleman informing them that he would not accept the pastorate of Sixteenth Street Baptist Church. Dr. Coleman clearly was displeased with the attitude of the congregation, but it also seems that he was not prepared to leave his pastorate in Jacksonville.

Once again the congregation asked the Rev. Benjamin A. Hawkins to assume the responsibility of being interim pastor until they could secure a full-time pastor.

TOPPING THE ROOF

● ● ● ● ● ● ●

On January 1, 1945, the congregation of Sixteenth Street Baptist Church called the Rev. Dr. Luke Beard, who was then serving New Hope Baptist Church in Meridian, Mississippi. Educated at Jackson College (now Jackson State University) and Lincoln University, Dr. Beard was highly respected as a leader, preacher, and teacher.

When Dr. Beard began his sixteen-year tenure at Sixteenth Street Baptist Church, the congregation numbered 900 members. The membership experienced continued growth under Dr. Beard's leadership, a testimony to the community's fondness for

The Rev. Dr. Luke Beard, Pastor 1945–1960

him. Like several of his predecessors, Dr. Beard faced the obstacle of being constantly challenged by some members of the church. Minutes of church conferences, as recorded by the clerk and approved by the congregation, often reflect a negative attitude toward Dr. Beard and his efforts to move Sixteenth Street Baptist Church in the direction he thought best.

Dr. Beard insisted that the congregation continue to sponsor community programs, and during his tenure a number of outside groups used the church facility for concerts and other gatherings. Conference minutes from this period indicate that the congregation wanted to protect its facility, and the custodial committee was consulted often about the number of times the church was being used and the impact of such use on the facility. Although the congregation did not have a clear preventive maintenance plan, whenever a problem arose the membership rallied its efforts to correct it.

Easter Sunday 1945

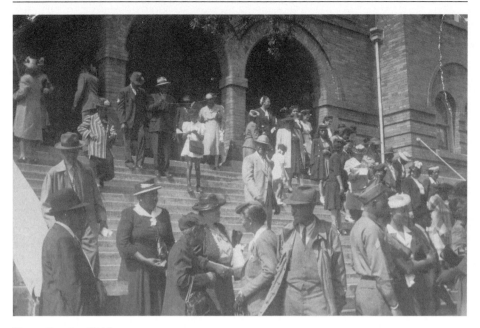

Easter Sunday 1945

During Dr. Beard's pastorate Birmingham's population, which had grown to 340,000, was fractured, divided racially both socially and politically. Very few black citizens were willing to confront this atrocious system, and none of the conference minutes or other historical records of Sixteenth Street Baptist Church from this period reflect a major concern on the part of the congregation about the racist atmosphere in the city. Congregational meetings did not, at least not officially, include discussions about segregated housing, businesses being confined to Fourth Avenue North—or any other racial issues. Seemingly all was well as far as Sixteenth Street Baptist Church was concerned, with the exception of the internal scrimmages that continued to plague the congregation.

In this regard, Sixteenth Street Baptist Church reflected the attitude of many congregations and black communities that had created self-contained environments. Rather than focusing on racial issues, the church focused on educational achievements. The congregation had always encouraged its young people to excel academically, and during Dr. Beard's tenure they placed emphasis on starting a scholarship fund to help students earn college degrees. Many of the church's members were teachers, lawyers, bankers, physicians, musicians, and other professionals. Outsiders considered members of Sixteenth Street Baptist Church to be the "Silk Stocking" congregation, the "Blue Bloods" of Birmingham. While such descriptions were not altogether true, that is how Birmingham's citizens perceived the church, and perceptions are difficult to change.

Despite the congregation's deliberate avoidance of racial issues, the members of Sixteenth Street Baptist Church lived in a racist city. In his 1954 book *South of Freedom*, Carl T. Rowan said that "Birmingham, Alabama, is the capital of Jim Crowism in America. Birmingham, industry's Pittsburgh of the South, is Jim Crow in birth, life, and death. It is, with apologies to Johannesburg and Capetown, South Africa, the world's most race-conscious city."

In Birmingham the realities of racism were especially highly visible and cruel. Racial consciousness was evident in every stratum of life for Birmingham's black citizens, and it was demanded by whites. Birmingham typified the racist attitude toward blacks throughout the South that was obvious in segregated seating and waiting rooms, and blacks being served through back doors at commercial businesses or not being served at all.

Easter Sunday 1945

When the Rev. Fred Lee Shuttlesworth, an influential, outspoken "country" preacher born on a farm in Mount Meigs, Alabama, became pastor of Bethel Baptist Church in Birmingham in 1953, he immediately began to think about ways to end the city's blatant racism. The Reverend Shuttlesworth became involved in the National Association for the Advancement of Colored People (NAACP) upon accepting the pastorate of Bethel Baptist Church, and later he became the NAACP's membership chairman.

When Alabama Attorney General John Patterson secured a court injunction on June 1, 1956, banning the NAACP in Alabama, the Reverend Shuttlesworth decided to defy the injunction. On June 4th he joined with other ministers to organize the Alabama Christian Movement for Human Rights (ACMHR) and became the leader of the Birmingham Civil Rights Movement that would confront systemic racism in Birmingham. The goals of the newly formed ACMHR were "freedom and democracy and the removal from our society of any form of second-class citizenship."

The following day, June 5, more than 1,000 people gathered at Sardis Baptist Church in Birmingham for a mass rally, with the Rev. R. L. Alford of Sardis Baptist Church, the Rev. N. H. Smith of New Pilgrim Baptist Church, and the Reverend Shuttlesworth as the featured speakers. This meeting signaled a new opportunity to advance the cause of ending segregation in Birmingham.

In establishing the ACMHR, the Reverend Shuttlesworth clearly stated that its methodology would be radically different from that of the NAACP, the pioneer Civil Rights organization. He believed that the NAACP was not aggressive enough in its stance against segregationists in the South, especially in Birmingham. He also knew that many Birmingham blacks did not fully support the local chapter of the NAACP because it was controlled by black professionals.

The Reverend Shuttlesworth incorporated the tenets of Walter Rauschenbush's social gospel theology early in the development of the ACMHR. The Reverend Shuttlesworth knew the Rev. Dr. Martin Luther King Jr. from his days in Selma, Alabama, and while Dr. King served as pastor of Dexter Avenue Baptist Church in Montgomery.

For America, no voice stands out stronger and louder in the Civil Rights Movement than that of the Rev. Dr. Martin Luther King Jr. Born in the capital of the New South, Atlanta, Georgia, Dr. King saw firsthand the discrimination inflicted against African Americans. As the son of a prominent pastor, Dr. King heard messages of liberation preached from the pulpit of Ebenezer Baptist Church and many other churches located near his home and church on Auburn Avenue.

Dr. King prepared himself for the leadership role that he would later assume by entering Morehouse College in Atlanta in 1944 and by putting himself under the spiritual influence of Dr. Benjamin E. Mays. At Morehouse he struggled with career choices. His grades in science courses precluded his decision to pursue medicine, and initially he attempted not to consider ministry. As David J. Garrow explains in *Bearing the Cross: Martin Luther King Jr. and the Southern Christian Leadership Conference*, Dr. King "was decidedly ambivalent about that course. Much black religion, he believed, emphasized emotion rather than ideas and volume rather than elocution." In 1947, however, Dr. King decided to pursue a career in ministry, and he was ordained by his father on February 25, 1948.

The "Voice of the Civil Rights Movement," as Dr. King became known, was influenced by his studies at Crozer Theological Seminary in Chester, Pennsylvania (now merged with Colgate Rochester Divinity School and Bexley Hall in Rochester, New York). There he studied the social gospel movement of Walter Rauschenbush, who argued that the role of religion is to confront social problems and that the church must be at the forefront of those issues. Rauschenbush believed that the Industrial Age exemplified in the North and the period of slavery in the South had caused rampant oppression unlike anything ever experienced in America. His theology of God's involvement in human affairs called upon Christians (and even non-Christians) to eradicate those ills that deprived all oppressed people of human decency.

Dr. King debated within himself Rauschenbush's claim and the strong influence of Reinhold Niebuhr's assessment that humanity's selfishness was a barrier to a just society. When Dr. King heard Dr. Mordecai Johnson, then president of Howard University, talk about revolutionary changes in India brought about by Mahatma Gandhi's movement, he also became influenced by Gandhi's pacifism. Dr. King's initial thoughts later were further modified by his studies at Boston University.

Dr. King's scholarly pursuits prepared him well for the pastorate of the Dexter Avenue Baptist Church in Montgomery, which was steeped with segregation. The public transportation system in Montgomery maintained a code of segregation against African Americans. On December 1, 1955, Rosa Parks, a seamstress, refused to move from the "no-Negro person's-land" section of a public bus. The bus driver hailed a police officer, who arrested Parks for violating the city code. This singular event caused Montgomery ministers and leaders to meet in the basement of Dexter Avenue Baptist Church to develop a response to Parks's arrest.

As Leah Rawls Atkins, Wayne Flynt, William Warren Rogers, and Robert David Ward point out in their 1994 book *Alabama: The History of a Deep South State*, "Black theology carried a strong tradition of liberation and social uplift. Black ministers also constituted one of the few groups in the community not dependent upon whites for their job."

Local black congregations empowered their ministers to provide the leadership for the Civil Rights Movement that others were prevented from providing. Dr. King's recent arrival in Montgomery made him a viable candidate for leadership, and the arrest of Rosa Parks and the galvanizing of all the incidents of racism in Montgomery made it possible for him to accept the prominent role of the leader for the Civil Rights Movement, a role that allowed him to put to practical test the ideas of Rauschenbush, Niebuhr, Gandhi, and other leaders he had studied in college and seminary.

Dr. King was elected president of the Montgomery Improvement Association, the organization that provided leadership for the Montgomery bus boycott in 1955. On November 13, 1955, the United States Supreme Court ruled that segregation on buses was unconstitutional. On December 21, 1956, thirteen months after Rosa Parks refused to give her seat to a white passenger, blacks boarded integrated buses in Montgomery.

Like Dr. King in Montgomery, the Reverend Shuttlesworth took a courageous stance against the atrocity of segregation in Birmingham. The Reverend Shuttlesworth possessed the understanding of the South's race problem necessary to shape a mass movement that would make a difference in Birmingham. The impetus for his action was prompted not only by the ousting of the NAACP in June 1956 but also by displays of a vicious brand of racism by Birmingham Public Safety Commissioner Eugene "Bull" Connor.

It is important to note that not all black ministers in Birmingham supported the efforts of the Reverend Shuttlesworth and the new ACMHR organization. When the Reverend Shuttlesworth moved to Birmingham, he immediately had begun to spark change in a city where many prominent ministers had been serving for years. Some ministers felt that the Reverend Shuttlesworth's style of leadership would lead to violence. Civil Rights lawyers Arthur D. Shores and

Bethel Baptist Church and parsonage, the home of the Rev. Fred L. Shuttlesworth, was bombed on Christmas Day 1956.

Orzell Billingsley Jr., a member of Sixteenth Street Baptist Church, "preferred the legal methods of the NAACP. The religious aspects of the new movement also turned some blacks away from the ACMHR," reported Dorothy Sterling in her 1968 book *Tear Down the Walls! A History of the American Civil Rights Movement.*

Birmingham had defied all the mandates of the Supreme Court and common sense. Strongly influenced by state politics and the menacing rage of the Ku Klux Klan, Birmingham became the worst place for blacks to live. As Sterling wrote in *Tear Down the Walls!*, "One hundred years after the Emancipation Proclamation, Birmingham's laws forbade 'the mixing of the races' in any public place." Birmingham's schools were still segregated, and the city had closed its parks, playgrounds, and golf courses instead of integrating them. When the manager of Birmingham's bus station desegregated the facility's lunch counter, the Birmingham police arrested him. Public accommodations from drinking fountains to taxis to health facilities bore White and Colored labels.

Displays of violence were commonplace in Birmingham, and bombings throughout black communities were not unusual. In his book *Bull Connor* William A. Nunnelley reports, "Between April 1956 and December 1957, seven bombings of black homes occurred in North Birmingham."

Not only were black communities and facilities targeted, but Jewish synagogues also became prime targets of the Ku Klux Klan. Commissioner of Public Safety Bull Connor usually had prior knowledge of the Klan's activities and "supported" them simply by doing nothing to stop them. Fifty-four sticks of dynamite were discovered in a window of Temple Beth-El on Birmingham's southside on April 28, 1958. The bomb did not explode, but it clearly highlighted the level of hatred of some of the whites who lived in Birmingham.

By 1960 the growth of Birmingham's steel industry began to plummet, resulting in a declining number of jobs and escalating racism. According to David J. Garrow's book *Birmingham, Alabama, 1956–1963: The Black Struggle for Civil Rights*, "newly urbanized blacks in Birmingham found a social structure that segregated Negroes from employment opportunities." The great racial divide of Birmingham set the stage for what would become the most crucial period in both the city's racial nightmare and Sixteenth Street Baptist Church's history.

Dr. Beard, who had pastored the congregation of Sixteenth Street Baptist Church through the early years of the Civil Rights Movement, died on March 21, 1960, after a brief illness. The congregation did not observe an official time of mourning and evidently showed a very blah attitude toward his passing. The congregation met for its scheduled quarterly conference on March 30, 1960, but for some unknown reason there is no mention in the recorded minutes of Dr. Beard's passing until the end of the meeting. The meeting began as usual with a devotion, approval of minutes from the previous meeting, and then a lengthy discussion about an incorrect auditor's report. After the discussion, the Official Board recommended that the congregation cover the cost of Dr. Beard's funeral, but one of the members even questioned the amount of the expense ($1,010 according to the minutes). Before adjourning the congregation approved a motion to send a letter and a resolution to Mrs. Beard.

The minutes from the next church conference, held April 13, 1960, do not mention the late Dr. Beard or the effect of his passing on the congregation. The minutes do record that the moderator for the April 13 meeting stated that the letter and resolution from the congregation to Mrs. Beard were in the hands of the secretary for mailing.

Dr. Beard's pastorate of Sixteenth Street Baptist Church coincided with the last decade of consistent growth in Birmingham's population. The next pastor would face leading the most influential black church in Birmingham through the most turbulent period in the city's history.

The congregation repeated its past pattern of struggling to find a full-time pastor. Almost a year after Dr. Beard died, the congregation gathered for a special called meeting on March 14, 1961. The 132 members at that meeting affirmed calling the Rev. Fulton O. Bradley to become Sixteenth Street Baptist Church's pastor, but they requested that the Reverend and Mrs. Bradley visit the church before accepting the call.

The Reverend and Mrs. Bradley visited Sixteenth Street Baptist Church during the congregation's eighty-eighth anniversary celebration in April 1961. The Pulpit Committee requested that the Reverend Bradley begin his duties by the first of July and not later than July 10th. On April 21, 1961, the church received a letter from the Reverend Bradley stating that he agreed to serve as the pastor and to assume his new duties by July 10, 1961.

In a special called conference after worship on May 28, 1961, a letter of resignation from the Reverend Bradley was read to the congregation. He said that the congregation he was serving had voted unanimously not to accept his resignation. The Reverend Bradley further stated that the Dean of Religion at Howard University had requested he consider staying on the faculty of the school.

Although devastated again by the action of a pastor who acknowledged and then reneged on his intent to come to Sixteenth Street Baptist Church, the congregation reactivated the pulpit committee. After several efforts to call various ministers, the congregation met January 17, 1962, and voted to call the Rev. John H. Cross. The Reverend Cross accepted, and in June 1962 he became the eleventh pastor of Sixteenth Street Baptist Church.

With great expectations the Reverend Cross, a native of Forrest City, Arkansas, left the church he was serving in Richmond, Virginia, and walked into Sixteenth Street Baptist Church and into the City of Birmingham whose racist tantrums would be broadcast across the wires of the world. The Reverend Cross understood the complexity of Birmingham, and his patient and inspiring influence would serve Sixteenth Street Baptist Church well at a most pivotal moment in its history.

As with church records from previous years, the minutes of church conferences held during this period fail to reflect the larger issues surfacing in the streets of Birmingham. Although members of the church lived and worked in various communities in Birmingham, there was never a statement made, or at least recorded, about the role of the Sixteenth Street Baptist Church in the wider community.

Reading the official minutes of church conferences, one gets the impression that Sixteenth Street Baptist Church remained an island unto itself. With the facility in close proximity to downtown businesses, the members were acutely aware of mistreatment in retail stores that discriminated against blacks. Many members of the congregation worked for the Birmingham School Board and taught in segregated schools. They knew Bull Connor and the brutal tactics of the Birmingham Police Department. They heard the bombs exploding around the city and in their neighborhoods. They read the papers, both black and white. They listened to the radio stations, both black and white. Members of the congregation continued to talk with each other outside of church, yet there is no mention of Birmingham's racist behavior in any of the minutes of the church. No discussion. No plans of intervening on behalf of black people. No theological discussions about freedom under God took place during congregational meetings at Sixteenth Street Baptist Church.

At the end of the Civil Rights campaign in Albany, Georgia, in fall 1962, the Reverend Shuttlesworth and others met with Dr. King in Georgia to develop strategies for the campaign in Birmingham. It was decided that Dr. King would come to Birmingham and provide leadership in partnership with the existing leadership.

The Reverend Shuttlesworth, Dr. King, the Rev. Wyatt Tee Walker, and others met at Gaston Motel on Fifth Avenue North and Sixteenth Street and developed "Project C (Confrontation)," their brain child strategy that would be used to address the racism prevalent in Birmingham and become a model of civil disobedience. It would become the best test case for Dr. King's theology of nonviolence. "Its goal was an 'open city' where all public services and facilities would be open to Negroes equally with whites," states Dorothy Sterling in *Tear Down the Walls!*

The Rev. John H. Cross, Pastor 1962–1968

50

The Rev. Fred L. Shuttlesworth, the Rev. Ralph Abernathy, Dr. Martin Luther King Jr., the Rev. Andrew Young, and other leaders of the Civil Rights Movement at Gaston Motel in 1963

Civil Rights planning meetings previously had been held in various Birmingham churches, including First Baptist Church Ensley, where the Rev. A. D. King (Dr. Martin Luther King's brother) served as pastor, and Bethel Baptist, where the Reverend Shuttlesworth served. For the mass meetings that were being planned as part of Project C, however, a larger and more convenient meeting place was needed. Sixteenth Street Baptist Church provided the ideal setting.

Although the minutes of church conferences do not reflect any conversations between the Reverend Cross and Dr. King or the Reverend Shuttlesworth about getting permission to use the church, mass meetings were held there. Initially the congregation did not want to become that involved because of previous bombings and horror stories, but the Reverend Cross insisted that it was Sixteenth Street Baptist Church's responsibility to do what it had always done by offering its facility to the community. Although several members expressed their dissatisfaction, the majority of the congregation agreed that the church would be used as the home for the Birmingham Civil Rights campaign.

The first publicly announced mass meeting held at Sixteenth Street Baptist Church brought with it all the horrors that the congregation expected. Bomb threats became an everyday occurrence, and the church's leadership grew very concerned about how the potential dangers would impact the church's ministry and the safety of its people.

The Reverend Cross and his family received many threatening calls and letters and often took temporary refuge away from the parsonage. Even though the parsonage was never attacked, the threats gave everyone cause for concern. During this fearful period, volunteers from various congregations and the community rotated security vigils throughout the night around Birmingham churches and in neighborhoods where the Civil Rights Movement leaders lived. As William A. Nunnelley reported in *Bull Connor*, the Reverend Cross and others didn't underestimate the extremists in Birmingham. "We've known right along there were people in this town capable of anything," said the Reverend Cross.

Similar to the 1955 call for action in Montgomery, a call for mass rallies went out in 1963 in the City of Birmingham to confront "Jim Crow" laws that existed in public transportation and accommodations. Under the leadership of the Reverend Shuttlesworth and others, black citizens expressed outrage at the oppressive way that the white power structure in Birmingham dehumanized them.

Initially the Reverend Shuttlesworth, Dr. King, and the other Civil Rights Movement leaders found it difficult to get full support from Birmingham's black citizens. The turning point came in April 1963 when Dr. King was incarcerated in a Birmingham jail for nine days.

On April 12, 1963, eight prominent white clergy of Birmingham and the metropolitan area sent Dr. King a letter requesting an end to the protest marches. From their perspectives, they had all to lose. They called Dr. King an outsider and viewed him as hostile to the kind of progress they deemed necessary for the City of Birmingham. Their white parishioners were voicing displeasure in coming downtown to the sight of blacks marching and demanding service in segregated businesses. They chose not to face the issue of justice but emphasized instead the need to solve race problems through amicable means. Like others, Birmingham's white clergy wanted to eat at department store counters. The economic threat was real, and they appealed to Dr. King for sensibility.

Dr. King responded to their letter with his famous April 16, 1963, "Letter From Birmingham City Jail." That letter stated in clear, eloquent, theological and philosophical terms why blacks could not end the protest marches. Dr. King reminded the white clergymen that in centuries past the Christian church had often proclaimed its boldest message from behind prison walls. In response to their call for "restraint and patience," Dr. King reminded them that "blacks had already waited 340 years for justice." Dr. King "pledged to honor laws he considered just but vowed to disobey ones he believed to be unjust."

The white clergymen did not respond to Dr. King's letter.

The Birmingham Civil Rights campaign succeeded largely because Bull Connor openly expressed the opinion that existed in the State of Alabama and generally across the South, the opinion that blacks were inferior to whites and that segregation was inherently good. At every level Connor did his best to make sure that blacks were controlled and kept "in their place."

As William A. Nunnelley states in *Bull Connor,* "Connor, facing Shuttlesworth for the first time in the commission setting, chastised the ACMHR leader for doing 'more to set your people back than any man in the history of this city.' Shuttlesworth accompanied by a delegation of forty-two blacks, retorted that 'history will have to decide whether I have done more to set them back or bring them forward.' " It was the Reverend Shuttlesworth's goal to confront Connor and the social ill that viewed blacks as everything but equal to whites.

The mass demonstrations continued throughout 1963. May 2, 1963, was a critical day in the movement for liberation from Birmingham's oppressive dehumanization. The Reverend Shuttlesworth, Dr. King, and the other leaders decided to incorporate children into the protest movement. Instead of attending school, young people came to Sixteenth Street Baptist Church and St. Paul United Methodist Church to receive training in civil disobedience from the Rev. James Bevel, Dorothy Cotton, and others. After receiving their instructions they left Sixteenth Street Baptist Church to begin their freedom walk.

Unlike anything that had happened before, Bull Connor ordered that the children be arrested. More than 500 young people were loaded in police vehicles and hauled to jail. But Connor did not anticipate that more children would become involved in the campaign. Even after the jails were filled, children continued to stream out of Sixteenth Street Baptist Church and attempt to march through Kelly Ingram Park, a "no-Negro person's-land" for protesters. Connor called for dogs and fire hoses. This event caused many parents whose participation had waned, to become involved in the movement.

The children's campaign succeeded in nationalizing the Birmingham Civil Right Movement. On May 3, 1963, both young people and adults filed from the sanctuary of Sixteenth Street Baptist Church to be met by the Birmingham

Police and Fire Departments. Bull Connor was forced to treat the children as he had earlier treated the adults who participated in mass rallies. He ordered that both the children and adults be fired upon with water hoses and viciously attacked by snarling dogs.

On May 7 1963, about 2,500 men, women, and children took to the streets of Birmingham, where Bull Connor and his troops met them. " 'Turn on your water, turn loose your dogs, we will stand here till we die,' a minister cried," recorded Dorothy Sterling in *Tear Down the Walls!*

In *Parting the Waters: America in the King Years, 1954–63*, Taylor Branch stated that Dr. King eased the concern of many parents at a rally by encouraging them not to worry about their children who had been subjected to fire hoses, police dogs, and arrest. "They are suffering for what they believe, and they are suffering to make this nation a better nation," said Dr. King.

One member of our congregation who was arrested in 1963 tells about being held in quarters with 200 others. Often days and even weeks would pass before parents could locate their children.

The Ku Klux Klan retaliated for the mass demonstrations by bombing black facilities throughout the city. Civil Rights attorney Arthur Shores lived in a neighborhood that was bombed so frequently throughout the spring of 1963, it became known as "Dynamite Hill." The homes of the Reverend Shuttlesworth and the Rev. A. D. King were also bombed. A bomb also exploded at Gaston Motel, owned by a local businessman A. G. Gaston who offered it as Dr. King's base of operations. With so many bombings that spring, people began calling Birmingham "Bombingham."

The events of spring 1963 in Birmingham reflected what was happening in other southern states. On April 23, 1963, William Lewis Moore, a postman from Baltimore, was shot and killed as he walked through Alabama during a one-man march against segregation. In Mississippi a sniper shot and killed Medgar Evers, who directed NAACP operations in Mississippi, was leading a campaign for integration in Jackson.

By late summer 1963, however, the leaders of the Birmingham Civil Rights Movement began to feel some optimism. The NAACP had been instrumental in winning a number of major court cases, and although there were many negative events plaguing the movement, there were also moments of great success. On June 23, 1963, King had led a march in Detroit, Michigan, that had attracted

Birmingham police officers used violation of the occupancy ordinance as their reason to break up a Civil Rights meeting at Sixteenth Street Baptist Church in 1963.

thousands. The City of Birmingham's government had changed from being controlled by commissioners to a mayor and council organization.

A. Phillip Randolph, a revered Civil Rights statesman, had organized a mass meeting to be held in Washington, D.C., on August 28, 1963. The goal was to bring thousands of people, black and white, to the seat of national power, and more than 250,000 met in front of the Lincoln Monument to hear a variety of speakers and singers. The crowning moment of that mass meeting Dr. King's "I Have A Dream" speech. In his speech, the last one he would ever give, Dr. King painted a vision of a new America that all citizens could embrace. In tones echoing the prophetic voices of the eighth century, Dr. King challenged America to live up to its creed and hold in trust the ideals of the Constitution of the United States of America.

The March on Washington was a fitting end to the bitter and violent summer of 1963.

The bomb that exploded on September 15, 1963, at Sixteenth Street Baptist Church blasted the face of Jesus Christ out of the rose window and shattered other stained-glass windows in the sanctuary.

SHATTERED WINDOWS

• • • • • •

The success of the March on Washington in August 1963, along with several local initiatives that demonstrated Birmingham was moving in the right direction toward integration, prompted Sixteenth Street Baptist Church and many of the city's black neighborhoods to relax their volunteer security patrols. No one, not even members of Sixteenth Street Baptist Church, was prepared on Sunday, September 15, 1963, to experience the worst atrocity of the Civil Rights Movement.

The Reverend Cross describes that day as a typical calm Sunday. Ethelda Finch, a member of Sixteenth Street Baptist Church who was a young girl at the time, recalled it being a "usual day—get up, get ready to go to church; put on your white because it's Youth Day; got to go to Sunday School."

The young people were to serve as worship leaders during the 11 a.m. service, and they came to church that Sunday morning dressed in their finest. The young ladies wore white dresses, and the young men wore black slacks and white shirts with black ties. The Reverend Cross had planned to preach from Matthew 25:31-46 and had titled his sermon "A Love That Forgives."

But the young people did not lead the 11 a.m. worship service on Sunday, September 15, 1963, and the Reverend Cross never preached that sermon.

J. S. Goodson, a retired educator and Deacon of Sixteenth Street Baptist Church, remembered his Sunday School class discussing the morning's lesson until "we heard that noise, and that noise boomed like a cannon." The noise came at 10:22 a.m. when approximately nineteen sticks of dynamite exploded under the exterior stairs on the northeastern side of the church.

Minutes after the explosion the Reverend Cross exited Sixteenth Street Baptist Church through a gaping hole in the lower-level wall and asked the concerned citizens who were gathering to remain calm and return to their homes. Many of the blacks listened and did what the pastor asked, but others shouted their dismay and began throwing rocks at any cars passing by with whites inside.

A white law enforcement officer, in full gear, stands ready to maintain order after the bomb exploded at the church. In 1963 blacks could serve as civil defense workers but not as policemen.

*Rescue workers found Addie Mae Collins, Denise McNair, Carole Robertson, Cynthia Wesley,
and Sarah Collins buried in the debris of what was the ladies lounge area in the church basement.*

The Reverend Cross and members of the congregation led the white policemen and paramedics who had arrived on the scene into the church basement.
There they discovered the bodies of fourteen-year-old Addie Mae Collins, eleven-
year-old Denise McNair, fourteen-year-old Carole Robertson, and fourteen-
year-old Cynthia Wesley. The lifeless bodies of the four young ladies were
rushed to Hillman Hospital (now University Hospital, part of the University of
Alabama at Birmingham), where they were pronounced dead on arrival.

The rescue workers also heard moans and found Sarah Collins, Addie's
sister, buried alive in the debris in the church basement. Sarah too was rushed
to the hospital, where she remained for more than two months undergoing
surgery and recovering from her extensive injuries. Sarah lost the sight in her
right eye as a result of the explosion. Other people who were injured in the
explosion were treated at the hospital and released.

The death certificates prepared by Birmingham coroner J. O. Butler state that Addie Mae Collins, Denise McNair, Carole Robertson, and Cynthia Wesley came to their deaths "from a bomb blast at the Sixteenth Street Baptist Church, Birmingham, Alabama, by person or persons unknown, same being homicide."

The pictures of the girls included in the coroner's autopsy reports reveal the major damage the "bomb blast" had inflicted on their young bodies. A piece of brick had smashed Denise McNair's head. Cynthia Wesley's head had been crushed to the point of decapitation. Carole Robertson and Addie Mae Collins had suffered equally atrocious injuries. The weight of the debris and the impact of the explosion at Sixteenth Street Baptist Church had cost four angels their lives.

As news of the bombing spread, people from everywhere hurriedly sent telegrams and made telephone calls expressing their disbelief. A few callers expressed satisfaction with the bombing but said they regretted that only four blacks had been killed.

Carole Robertson's family held a funeral for her on Tuesday, September 17, at St. John A.M.E. Church. The Reverend Cross presided at Carole's funeral, which Frank Sikora describes in *Until Justice Rolls Down*.

The bomb blasted away the exterior wooden staircase and shot brick, mortar, and debris from the basement wall into the ladies lounge area of the church and onto cars parked on the street.

The September 15, 1963, bomb explosion killed four young ladies, injured twenty-two other people, and heavily damaged the Sixteenth Street Baptist Church facility.

Gazing down on the flower-banked casket, Cross spoke somberly: "This atrocious act was committed not against race, but against all freedom-loving persons in the world. Somehow, out of this dastardly act, we have been brought together again as never before. May we not seek revenge against those who are guilty, but find our refuge in love and the words of Paul, who said, "All things work together for good for those who love God."

White clergy in Birmingham joined with blacks in the funeral procession before the joint service for Denise McNair, Cynthia Wesley, and Addie Mae Collins on Wednesday, September 18, 1963, at Sixth Avenue Baptist Church. Dr. King preached the eulogy at the service and used the opportunity to

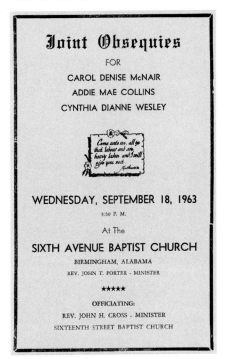

Joint Obsequies

FOR

CAROL DENISE McNAIR
ADDIE MAE COLLINS
CYNTHIA DIANNE WESLEY

WEDNESDAY, SEPTEMBER 18, 1963

3:30 P. M.

At The

SIXTH AVENUE BAPTIST CHURCH

BIRMINGHAM, ALABAMA

REV. JOHN T. PORTER · MINISTER

★★★★★

OFFICIATING:

REV. JOHN H. CROSS · MINISTER
SIXTEENTH STREET BAPTIST CHURCH

Carole Robertson's family held a separate funeral service for her on September 17th.

challenge the Birmingham community to work for reconciliation. Dr. King said that "we must not harbor the desire to retaliate with violence. The deaths may well serve as the redemptive force that brings light to this dark city." Dr. King later referred to the four young girls as "modern heroines of a holy crusade."

The bomb that exploded Sunday morning, September 15, 1963, at Sixteenth Street Baptist Church in Birmingham killed four young black girls, injured twenty-two other blacks, heavily damaged the church facility—and sent shock waves across America and around the world.

In *Until Justice Rolls Down* Frank Sikora wrote that in reflecting later upon the potential for violence against Sixteenth Street the Reverend Cross said, "We've been expecting this all along, waiting for it, knowing it would come, wondering when."

In an interview Walter Cronkite gave some thirty-five years after the bombing for Spike Lee's documentary *4 Little Girls*, the former *CBS News* anchor said that whites across America didn't really understand the "real nature of the hate that was preventing integration" until the "incredibly mean, perverted, terrible crime of blowing up kids in a Sunday school basement" occurred. The bombing of Sixteenth Street Baptist Church "was the awakening."

When news about the bombing, the death of the four young girls, and the damage to Sixteenth Street Baptist Church reached Wales in the United Kingdom, the children of Cardiff began a "penny campaign" to raise money to replace one of the church's broken stained-glass windows. When the businessmen of Cardiff learned about the children's efforts, they decided to commission John Petts, a noted stained-glass craftsman and passionate artist, to design the replacement window.

To gain a better understanding of this human tragedy, Petts came to Birmingham to meet with the Reverend Cross and the members of Sixteenth Street Baptist Church and discuss possible designs. When Petts returned to his studio in Cardiff, he created "The Wales Window for Alabama," a multicolored window featuring a Jesus of African heritage whose large hands are extended in revolutionary protest and God's reconciling love. Petts based his image of

Welsh stained-glass artist John Petts's preliminary drawing for "The Wales Window for Alabama"

From John Petts, Cambria House, Llanstephan, Carmarthenshire, Wales, Gt.Britain

To the Revd. John Cross, 16th Street Baptist Church, 1530 North Sixth Avenue,
Birmingham, Alabama 35204

28th May 1965

My Dear John,

My warm thanks to you and Mrs Leanna Parchman for your wonderful
letter this morning which made us very happy here. It is most reassuring to
know that the window, on which we lavished so much loving care here in our
studio-workshop, has completed its long journey safely, and is about to take.
its intended place at last in your Church. We would, of course, love to
be there with you all for the Service of Dedication on Sunday, 6th June,
but unfortunately our work here for other churches makes this impossible.
I am sure you will understand. However, you will know that we shall be with
you in spirit and feeling on that day, and we shall look forward to hearing
news of the great occasion. Will there be documentary records made in sound
and on film ?   It would be a fine thing is this could be arranged, for then
we could all see and hear it over here.

A further word on the window. The great idea it seeks to express is
the identification of Christ and Everyman. In the face of the huge world problem
of intolerance, the denial of human rights, hatred, violence of man against
man, colour-bars and segregation, the simple words of Christ stand out: 'You
Do It to ME...'   The arrow and the bar of the Cross stands for the Spear in
the Side,all violence and suffering.   Surely the core of Christ's message is
what each man does to his neighbour, and the answer to the question 'Who is
my neighbour?'

Perhaps you will be asked about the significance of the large hands
of the figure in the window. They are emphasised in this way to express strongly
the meaning of the crucified gesture of the wide figure. One hand is strong
in protest, the other is wide in acceptance and love.   The Rainbow, forming
a nimbus, is the Light of the World, and the unity of all colours, and God's
Promise and Covenant.   The background colours of rich blues and purples
symbolise suffering and hope. Blue, as you will know, traditionally stands for
divine contemplation, love of divine works, piety, sincerity, loyalty, fidelity,
faith, humility and expiation. It signifies also eternity and immortality.

I would like at this time to send a message to you all: OUR
DEEPLY-FELT WISH THAT THIS WINDOW WILL STAND HIGH IN YOUR CHURCH FOR MANY YEARS
TO COME, ITS COLOURS SHINING WITH THE GLORY OF THE GREAT SIMPLE TRUTH WHICH
MUST PREVAIL: THAT ALL MEN ARE BROTHERS, AND THAT GOD IS LOVE.

My family, my wife and the children, join me in sending warm
greetings to yours.

All regards and good wishes, always,

Yours very sincerely,

John Petts

Jesus on a picture he had seen of a black protester taking part in a street
demonstration in the South. The man's arms were flung above his head, and his
body was gyrating as he was assaulted with fire hoses. The Jesus in the window
Petts designed symbolized the crucified Christ and forms the upright beam of a
cross, while a stylized stream of water from a fire hose forms the cross beam.

Petts wanted to connect the Birmingham Civil Rights Movement with the ongoing struggle in South Africa and thereby symbolize oppression everywhere. So he painted bullets onto the top beam of the cross to represent the innocent children and adults being gunned down in Sharpeville, South Africa, and other places in the world. He used a rainbow-colored nimbus on the Christ figure in his window to symbolize that God loves every person equally without respect to nationality, race, or creed—for we are one in Christ Jesus. At the bottom of the window, Petts placed the words of Christ, the words that the Reverend Cross had intended to say in the sermon he did not give on Sunday, September 15, 1963: "You Do It To Me."

The loss of the lives of four innocent young black girls killed by the bomb at Sixteenth Street Baptist Church and two young black boys killed while playing in the streets of Birmingham the day the bomb exploded, the injuries inflicted on other members of Sixteenth Street Baptist Church, and the heavy damage to the facility initiated havoc and resounding cries for restitution. The revolution that had begun with organized mass rallies denouncing Birmingham's segregation laws, Commissioner of Public Safety Eugene "Bull" Connor's actions, and daily threats against blacks had come to a major intersection with the bombing of Sixteenth Street Baptist Church. In "Death in the Morning," an article she wrote for the Fall 1982 issue of *Down Home* magazine, Dr. Geraldine Watts Bell stated that "there are few, if any, incidents of such magnitude and unspeakable savagery, that occurred during the civil rights movement that touched so many people all over the world."

Sixteenth Street Baptist Church, the facility designed by blacks, built by blacks, and supported by blacks, sat in ruins, stillness, and horror. The bomb had cast an ugly shadow on the thriving congregation that had allowed its facility to house the Birmingham Civil Rights Movement.

Local newspaper reporter Frank Sikora said that "the bombing of the Sixteenth Street Baptist Church stood out for several reasons—the first being, of course, that it was not just a terror tactic but a homicidal event." Sikora continues by saying:

The amount of explosives used at the church was far greater than at other targets. For instance, when New Bethel Baptist Church was bombed on January 16, 1962, there was only one stick of dynamite used. There were six sticks used at Bethel Baptist Church when it was bombed on December 14, 1962, slightly injuring two infants. Six sticks were also used at the Gaston Motel and at the residence of King's brother, A. D. King, both of which were bombed on May 11, 1963.

The home of Attorney Shores was bombed twice within a two-week period in 1963, with two sticks of dynamite used in each case. But at the Sixteenth Street Baptist Church, between ten and twenty sticks of dynamite were detonated, and when they went off they did more than just scare some blacks.

From October through December 1963 the congregation of Sixteenth Street Baptist Church received more than $280,000, $47,309.71 from an insurance policy held by the church and the rest from donations. The congregation established three distinct accounts to receive and disburse funds, a Building Fund, Bereaved Families Fund, and an Education Fund. According to T. L. Crowell, who audited the three accounts, the Education Fund received $12,061.79 in donations, a total of $24,172.24 in donations was distributed to the four families, and $217,328.75 from the insurance money and donations was used to repair the sanctuary and lower auditorium.

Until the repairs were completed in June 1964, the Reverend Cross and church officials used the old parsonage next to the bombed church building as an office. The congregation held worship services in nearby L. R. Hall Auditorium and meetings in Poole Funeral Home.

At a meeting on November 19, 1963, the congregation voted to purchase two additional lots facing Sixth Avenue North and construct an educational building on the property. The proposed facility would contain recreational facilities as well as educational space for classes. The congregation agreed to accept the offer of an architectural firm to design for free the educational building and the renovations that would be incorporated in repairing the sanctuary. The congregation voted to retain the services of L. S. Gaillard Jr., a member of the church, as general contractor for the building and restoration projects. The minutes of the meeting also record that the congregation acknowledged and was pleased to accept the generous offer from the people of Cardiff, Wales, to replace a stained-glass window that had been broken by the explosion.

Despite the enormous worldwide impact of the bombing, the pendulum of justice swung slowly in Birmingham even though officials suspected, if not knew, immediately after the bomb exploded who was responsible. Robert Chambliss, better known as "Dynamite Bob," was fingered to have been involved in or knowledgeable about most of the bombings that took place in and around Birmingham during the Civil Rights Movement.

Chambliss was a part of a Ku Klux Klan group called the "Cahaba Boys." In *Long Time Coming* Elizabeth H. Cobbs, Chambliss's niece, wrote, "This small Klan group, known as the 'Cahaba Boys,' has been given a great deal of attention in books, articles, and television documentaries. It has also been variously called Klavern 13 and the Cahaba Group. Klavern 13 was actually the chartered group that met in Woodlawn during the late fifties and early sixties; it had its own klokan, or secret militant-action group, as did all the klaverns."

According to Cobbs several members of Klavern 13 made up a core group of participants that were very involved in harassing blacks, and their methods were cruel, menacing, and vicious. "The group's membership shifted over the years, but the core group consisted of Robert [Chambliss], Troy Ingram, Thomas "Pop" Blanton (and later, his son Tommy, Jr.), latecomer Bobby Cherry, Herman and Jack Cash, Charles Cagle, John Wesley 'Nigger' Hall, Ross Keith, and a handful of others whose roles varied from starting fires to securing and hauling dynamite; building and placing bombs; providing

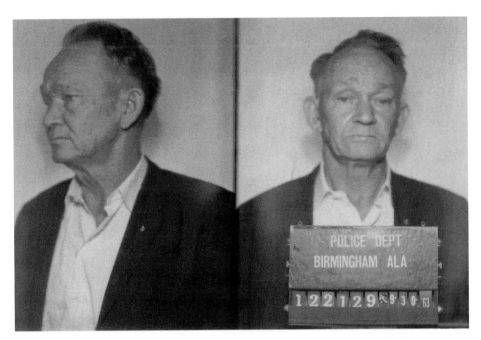

Robert Chambliss was found guilty of the murder of Denise McNair, one of the four bombing victims.

alibis, surveillance, and diversions; and just generally keeping track of each other."

While she was growing up Cobbs often visited the Chambliss home to spend time with her mother's sister, Flora "Tee" Chambliss. Cobbs saw Klansmen when they came to visit Robert Chambliss, and she heard a lot about the activities perpetrated by the Klan, especially Klavern 13's attack on black people. Her recollections would provide valuable information in 1977 when Chambliss would finally be convicted for the death of Denise McNair. Her words alone would eventually help the shattered pieces of Sixteen Street Baptist Church and Birmingham come together again.

During the 1977 trial Gertrude Glenn, an eyewitness who was visiting Birmingham from Detroit, testified that about 2 a.m. the morning of September 15, 1963, she had seen some white men sitting in a car parked near Sixteenth Street Baptist Church. Glenn said the light inside the car was on, and Chambliss looked like one of those men.

In his closing remarks at the 1977 trial, Alabama Attorney General Bill Baxley said that the bombing was a crime "against all of us, against the people of Birmingham and the state of Alabama." The jury found Chambliss guilty, and the judge sentenced him to life imprisonment. On February 20, 1978, Chambliss wrote a letter to Sixteenth Street Baptist Church contending that he was not responsible for the September 1963 bombing, and he continued to proclaim his innocence until the day he died in prison in 1985.

The pastor and congregation of Sixteenth Street Baptist Church had to harness spiritual strength to continue the church's ministry. The wide-reaching impact of the bombing, the loss of four innocent lives, the injuries of twenty-two other members, and the substantial damage inflicted on its historic facility forever changed the congregation's role in the community. The Reverend Cross guided Sixteenth Street Baptist Church through the shattered glass of Sunday, September 15, 1963, and helped the congregation see the bombing as an opportunity to redirect its energies for good.

In 1967 Claude Wesley, whose daughter Cynthia was killed in the bombing, recommended that Sixteenth Street Baptist Church join the Downtown Action Committee of Operation New Birmingham, which had been established as a means of communicating with area churches and businesses. Wesley also recommended that the Reverend Cross be the designated representative, and the congregation agreed.

This plaque, mounted on the wall of the Memorial Nook at Sixteenth Street Baptist Church, reminds everyone who sees it about the atrocious act of racial violence that took the lives of four innocent children on Sunday morning, September 15, 1963.

The congregation also took steps to make Sixteenth Street Baptist Church itself a memorial to help everyone remember the atrocious racist act of violence that took place here on September 15, 1963. As Maxine McNair, Denise's mother, said, "There are those who would like to brush this thing under the rug . . . but it happened. Those children are dead because of some fiendish act. We don't need to forget."

The Memorial Nook in the Lower Auditorium includes a plaque memorializing Addie Mae Collins, Denise McNair, Carole Robertson, and Cynthia Wesley. Thousands of visitors come to the church every year and pause in front of that plaque. It reminds them of the tragic loss of innocence—not just in Birmingham, but across the nation and around the world.

People who visit Sixteenth Street Baptist Church also pause in front of John Petts's "Wales Window for Alabama" to appreciate its message of hope.

"That Which Might Have Been: Birmingham, 1963," a sculpture by John Henry Waddell, is on permanent display at the Unitarian Church of Phoenix in Paradise Valley, Arizona.

In a letter to the Reverend Cross on May 28, 1965, Petts wrote about what he hoped the Wales Window would convey to the people who saw it.

> The great idea it seeks to express is the identification of Christ and Everyman. In the face of the huge world problem of intolerance, the denial of human rights, hatred, violence of man against man, colour-bars and segregation, the simple words of Christ stand out: "You Do It to Me." The arrow and the bar of the Cross stands for the Spear in the Side, all violence and suffering. Surely the core of Christ's message is what each man does to his neighbour, and the answer to the question "Who is my neighbour?"

Several poets and songwriters wrote special pieces that memorialize the bombing of Sixteenth Street Baptist Church. In 1964 Richard Farina wrote "Birmingham Sunday," and Joan Baez later recorded it for Vanguard Records. In 1965 Dudley Randall wrote "Ballad of Birmingham," a poem that is often quoted in reference to the loss of a daughter. A. L. Walsh also wrote a poem about the four young girls, and Estella Conwill Majozo dedicated the poem "Steps to the City" to the memory of the four girls.

Another artist, Arizona sculptor John Henry Waddell, and his family were returning from Mexico, where he had been teaching for two years, on Sunday, September 15, 1963. When they crossed the border into the United States they decided to tune the car radio to their favorite program but heard instead the news about the bombing of Sixteenth Street Baptist Church and the deaths of four young ladies. For some time Waddell had felt the need to do a sculpture that symbolized the Civil Rights struggle of black people in America. He internalized the shock of that Sunday morning's news report by envisioning four life-size figures based on the four young girls who had died in the bombing.

Waddell worked for a year on his four-figure grouping "That Which Might Have Been: Birmingham, 1963." The sculpture grouping is permanently displayed in a contemplative setting at the Unitarian Church of Phoenix in Paradise Valley, Arizona. Waddell's sculpture grouping has become a popular tourist site in Phoenix, and it is common to find visitors quietly sitting with the group or becoming a part of the group.

Waddell has explained the symbolism of the grouping. The "maternal" figure faces east, the beginning of day, and holds a swaddling cloth to represent the children she will never have. A figure caught in the act of turning faces south and represents the question of whether the American public will accept or reject African Americans. The figure facing west, the ending of day, represents the acceptance of death, love, help, and cooperation. The figure facing north has an upraised hand inscribed with the word "prayer" and represents hope. The open space in the center of the grouping represents a vortex, an uplifting flow of faith.

Waddell's sculpture was the first of a number of memorials dedicated to the bombing of Sixteenth Street Baptist Church and the memory of the four young ladies. When members of the First Baptist Church of Englewood, New Jersey, heard the news of the bombing, they decided to incorporate a fitting memorial into their building project. On Sunday, October 23, 1966, the Rev. J. Isaiah Goodman, pastor of the church, and members dedicated "The Chapel of the Four Children" in memory of Addie Mae Collins, Denise McNair, Carole Robertson, and Cynthia Wesley. The Reverend Goodman expressed the desire of his congregation not to dwell on the negative aspect of the bombing and the deaths of the four young girls but to use the chapel as a "prelude to a desire to make life beautiful in all its aspects, over and above the weak and thoughtless concept of the average thinker. It is our desire to point up all of the possibilities that are destined to bring life to its finest point of human existence."

This congregation made an intentional effort to remember the loss of four innocent children and the bombing of a church where children go to learn about love. The dedication of this chapel to their memories and the significant event of the bombing spoke volumes about the response that many people understood had to be made. During the dedication service the Reverend Goodman said:

> Memorializing these four children will not lighten the burden and respon-
> sibility of the human race; it is simply a reminder of the sacrifices that
> must be made in the light of progress. Because of their youth they could not
> know the importance of the great struggle for freedom. They were blessed
> with the guarantee of parental care and comfort. They did not feel the cold
> bleak air of servitude. They were not aware of the long, uphill journey since
> the days of slavery. But they were nevertheless to become an integral part
> of that struggle, and their lives have marked the pages of history in blood.
> The Chapel of the Four Children will stand as a monument to these four
> innocent girls, and we shall look upon it as a symbol of hope and an altar
> of faith.

A church in New York City has also dedicated a chapel to the memory of the four young girls. A church in East Orange, New Jersey, has dedicated a garden courtyard area to the four girls and the bombing of Sixteenth Street Church.

In 1974 the Carole Robertson Center for Learning was established on the west side of Chicago. The center, which is dedicated to memory of the four girls, has a mission of nurturing and challenging children and young people and supporting and strengthening families. The center provides day care, youth recreation, family support, counseling, child and family advocacy, and a variety of other programs for its more than 600 clients. In the early 1990s the Denise McNair Learning Center opened at Redeemer Lutheran Church in Oklahoma City, Oklahoma.

In 1992 Birmingham native sculptor John Rhoden gave the congregation of Sixteenth Street Baptist Church a large bronze plaque that depicts many events from 1963, including the Civil Rights rallies, marches, the fire hoses and police dogs, and the church bombing. Rhoden used the image of cutout dolls to represent the four young ladies killed in the bombing.

In her 1982 article Dr. Geraldine Bell, a former interim superintendent of Birmingham City Schools, stressed the need for the city's citizens to establish a permanent memorial to honor the deaths of the four girls and the sacrifices made by their families. "Although there are several memorials . . . in other states, there has been no significant effort on the part of Birmingham and Alabama citizenry to remember these sacrifices appropriately," said Bell.

In 1983 *The Birmingham News* established a scholarship fund in memory of the four girls to help educate deserving young people of Birmingham. Approximately 260 scholarships have been awarded from the fund since 1984.

After providing steady leadership for Sixteenth Street Baptist Church for six years the Reverend Cross sent a letter to the congregation giving his resignation effective June 2, 1968. The Reverend Cross's letter apparently was somehow lost, and the congregation was told at a special called meeting on April 17, 1968. The congregation established a pulpit committee to begin the process of identifying the next pastor.

The minutes that have been reconstructed from the recollections of some of the members present at that meeting do not reveal a specific negative reason for the Reverend Cross's resignation. Evidently the Reverend Cross did state that his mind was settled on the decision and that an offer of more money would not motivate him to change his mind. The Reverend Cross accepted a position with the Southern Baptist Convention and moved to Atlanta.

In the April 17 meeting, Deacon and longtime member Dr. W. C. Patton said that Sixteenth Street Baptist Church had a poor public image both locally and nationally. He expressed concern that the resignation of the Reverend Cross be handled with sincerity as a means of improving the church's image.

The renovated sanctuary of Sixteenth Street Baptist Church, September 1997

PICKING UP THE PIECES

• • • • • •

On the recommendation of the Pulpit Committee at a church conference on July 10, 1968, the congregation of Sixteenth Street Baptist Church extended a call to the Rev. James T. Crutcher to become its pastor. The Reverend Crutcher, a native of Kentucky, accepted the call and came to Birmingham after completing his B.D. (Master of Divinity) degree at Colgate Rochester Divinity School in Rochester, New York.

The Reverend Crutcher possessed the enthusiasm and courage to move Sixteenth Street Baptist Church beyond the 1963 bombing to its next stage of ministry. Sixteenth Street Baptist Church was poised for effective, wide-reaching ministry at the beginning of its second centennial, and the honor of this distinction forced the congregation to understand the significance of its facility in American history.

Early in his pastorate the Reverend Crutcher outlined an ambitious program for the congregation to consider. The first change he recommended and effected was to have the official minutes of church conferences be typed. He presented fifteen additional ideas that would enhance the congregation's ability to minister to the church's members and also become more involved in the community.

1. *Establish a thrift shop.*

2. *Assist in the housing program of the community.*

3. *Open a day-care center.*

4. *Develop a senior citizens club.*

5. *Create a lonely heart's club.*

6. *Establish a youth canteen.*

7. *Start a senior citizens nursing home.*

8. *Initiate a marriage clinic.*

9. *Open a credit union.*

10. *Institute voter registration classes and/or citizenship classes.*

11. *Employ a director of Christian education.*

12. *Sponsor Boy Scout and Girl Scout troops.*

13. *Conduct visitation and evangelism classes either person to person or using a block plan.*

14. *Undertake special projects including sewing classes, cooking classes, ceramics, art, hatmaking, photography, coffee house ministry, and family help with budgeting.*

15. *Provide help with personal and social adjustment for prospective workers on jobs.*

The congregation accepted and began to move on the Reverend Crutcher's fifteen ideas. In addition the congregation appointed a committee to organize a credit union. The congregation also organized the Economic Development Corporation of the Sixteenth Street Baptist Church, which was slated to be incorporated by Attorney Orzell Billingsley, with the primary goal of constructing a 200-unit apartment building, on Fifth Avenue North between Thirteenth and Seventeenth Streets, for the elderly of the community. The Economic Development Corporation is not mentioned in the minutes of any congregational conference after the July 16, 1969. The congregation evidently dropped the project and missed out on a golden opportunity to impact the city in a very positive way

In 1968 the congregation also reconsidered the project that had been approved on November 19, 1963, to build an educational building in honor of the four young ladies killed in the September 15th bombing. The congregation decided the educational building was still an attainable project.

The Rev. Dr. James T. Crutcher, Pastor 1968–1982

Under the Reverend Crutcher's leadership the congregation expanded existing programs, started new programs, and made outreach into the community a priority. The Reverend Crutcher saw a great need to establish a viable youth program and made it a top priority. The church membership already had enough young people and adult leadership to structure and maintain a strong youth ministry.

The young people readily accepted the Reverend Crutcher's interest and were excited about the potential that existed for them to become more involved in the ministry of their church. Thirty-eight of them served as the organizing members of the Baptist Youth Fellowship of Sixteenth Street Baptist Church. The first major hurdle the young people had to cross was getting permission to hold a dance in the Lower Auditorium of the church. Several adults expressed displeasure about holding such an event at the church, and in a subsequent meeting one of the church members made a motion that dancing never be allowed on church property. The Reverend Crutcher asked that a representative from the youth group speak to the congregation about the planned dance. After hearing James L. Lowe Jr. talk about what the youth planned to do, the majority of the adults present at the meeting voted to allow dancing on the church property for this one event.

Like many of the former pastors of Sixteenth Street Baptist Church, the Reverend Crutcher occasionally faced a brute antagonistic attitude of some members of the congregation at church conferences. No member of any church would dare say that any pastor is above constructive criticism or being questioned, but some members (many times the same people year after year) of Sixteenth Street Baptist Church publicly and disrespectfully criticized the leadership or authority of their pastor. Minutes of church conferences from this period frequently include statements such as "I suggest that all the power [bestowed] upon the Reverend Crutcher be taken from him and given back to the deacons and the church." Similar statements had been made in the past about former pastors of the church.

While Sixteenth Street was attempting to move forward in 1970 with a membership of approximately 525, the City of Birmingham experienced a loss of 11 percent of its population, a trend that would be repeated many times in the coming years. The total population for the city in 1970 was approximately 341,000, with a black population of 126,000. White flight into the southern suburbs was becoming a pattern that eventually led to black citizens becoming the majority of the city's population. Birmingham was bracing for major political changes.

During 1973, which marked the centennial of Sixteenth Street Baptist Church, the congregation took special steps to highlight its history and the role it was continuing to play in the changing City of Birmingham. Under the leadership of Mrs. Margery Gaillard, a memorial plaque bearing the pictures of Addie Mae Collins, Denise McNair, Carole Robertson, and Cynthia Wesley, the four young girls killed in the 1963 bombing, was placed on the wall of the sanctuary. The congregation also opened the doors of the church to the public on Wednesdays from noon to 4 p.m. so people from around the world could visit the site of the 1963 bombing and see the memorial plaque, the Wales Window for Alabama, and a number of historic church artifacts. Also the congregation approved having postcards of the Wales Window for Alabama and a Centennial souvenir plate produced for sale to the public.

In 1973 the Reverend Crutcher requested and received a semi-sabbatical leave to complete his Doctor of Ministry degree. The Reverend Crutcher made the commitment to return to Birmingham to preach on the first and third Sundays of each month during his semi-sabbatical, and the congregation asked the lay leadership of the church to preside at church conferences whenever the Reverend Crutcher was absent.

By the end of 1973 the congregation had experienced a net growth of five new members for a total of 491, which continued the pattern of steady decline of past years. The congregation made several attempts to explore increasing the membership through evangelistic efforts, but those meager efforts never proved too beneficial.

Recognizing that several members of the church were either being deliberately absent or had joined other churches, the congregation established a committee to investigate the status of inactive members. The active members placed a big emphasis on attempting to convince former members to return to Sixteenth Street Baptist Church.

In 1974 the congregation established a special committee to seriously evaluate the status of the former proposed educational building and give the congregation a recommendation about the need for it. The congregation also appointed a committee to investigate opening a day-care center in the Lower Auditorium of the church. The minutes of church conferences from this period, however, do not reflect any concrete decisions made about either project. Eventually the momentum to move forward with both the educational building and the day-care center would be lost due to lack of interest, lack of funds, and internal conflict between certain church members and the Reverend Crutcher. As it had several times before, the congregation of Sixteenth Street Baptist Church made the mistake of focusing on internal personality issues and in so doing lost sight of its mission as a church.

At a special called conference on Wednesday, March 10, 1976, the congregation learned that $12,141.05 had been missing from the church's checking account but, according to Treasurer Dr. J. S. Goodson, it had been put back into the account. It was speculated that the church secretary had forged checks, including one for $200 dated March 2, 1976. The congregation immediately appointed a personnel committee to screen future employees.

According to the minutes of the March 10, 1976, meeting, the Reverend Crutcher called for a motion to adjourn and upon failure to get one left. Mr. Bennie H. Wilson Sr., chairman of the Board of Deacons, presided over the remainder of the meeting. Some of the members expressed their concern about the subject matter being discussed, but the meeting continued.

One member critically exclaimed that Reverend Crutcher's seven and a half years as pastor had been a failure, and she made a motion to declare the pulpit vacant as of that evening. The motion was seconded and passed by a final vote of 43 to 38. It is important to emphasize that the majority of the church membership did not attend conferences, including this one, so the vote to dismiss the Reverend Crutcher did not necessarily represent the will of a large number of members. The members present at the meeting approved a motion to offer the Reverend Crutcher salary for ninety days if he agreed to vacate the pulpit. Several members were appointed to "serve" the pastor this offer.

In a special called meeting held Wednesday, March 24, 1976, the Reverend Crutcher heard a resolution outlining the method used to determine his employment status with the church. The Reverend Crutcher had successfully fought off one earlier recommendation for his dismissal. Evidently many of the church members still supported him because at the March 24th meeting when H. D. Coke made a motion that was seconded by J. L. Lowe Sr. "that Rev. James T. Crutcher be retained as pastor of the Sixteenth Street Baptist Church. The vote was 160 for and 1 against."

Strange as it may seem, the congregation involved the Jefferson County judicial system to resolve the issue of the Reverend Crutcher's dismissal. The litigation for resolving this conflict between Sixteenth Street Baptist Church and the Reverend Crutcher cost $2,681.76 in lawyers' fees and court costs. Perhaps more importantly, this internal strife proved costly for the church not only in terms of money but also in public embarrassment from newspaper accounts about the dispute. The court decided in favor of the Reverend Crutcher, and he remained as pastor of Sixteenth Street Baptist Church.

Until 1976 Sixteenth Street Baptist Church had been operating without a constitution or bylaws. In light of the embarrassing legal conflict between some of the church members and the Reverend Crutcher, the congregation asked Dr. Charles A. Brown Sr. to serve as leader of a committee to draft a constitution and bylaws to guide the congregation in resolving future conflicts.

Despite ongoing internal strife, outside groups continued to recognize the importance of Sixteenth Street Baptist Church. In 1976 the Jefferson County Historical Commission recognized the church especially for its historical worth. Also in 1976 the State of Alabama Register of Landmark and Heritage gave the church a historic marker that was placed on the southeast corner of the building. These two special recognitions alone clearly show that the physical structure of Sixteenth Street Baptist Church is of historic worth and should be preserved as such.

EXAMINING THE PIECES

● ● ● ● ● ●

The congregation of Sixteenth Street Baptist Church became involved in another kind of litigation in August 1977 when a grand jury was convened to hear testimony about the bombing on September 15, 1963. Unlike the court case between some members of the congregation and the Reverend Crutcher, this case opened fourteen-year-old wounds and revisited blighted images from the church's past. On November 18, 1977, at the courageous insistence of Alabama Attorney General Bill Baxley and after family member Elizabeth H. Cobbs, courageously turned state's evidence, the grand jury decided that there was enough evidence to charge Robert "Dynamite Bob" Chambliss with the murder of Denise McNair, one of the four young ladies killed when the bomb exploded.

The trial of Robert Chambliss revealed no new pertinent information—FBI agents had known almost all of the information in 1963. The only reason Chambliss had finally been brought to trial was that state investigator Bob Eddy had persisted in investigating the bombing and in winning the trust of Elizabeth Cobbs, who was very suspicious of both the FBI and the Birmingham Police Department. Cobbs knew that in 1963 many police officers in Birmingham and other parts of Alabama were affiliated with the Ku Klux Klan or had knowledge of the Klan's activities. In talking with Eddy, Cobbs finally revealed what she knew about her uncle, Robert Chambliss, and other members of the Klan.

> I told him I believed that Robert had, in fact, been involved in placing the bomb that exploded that Sunday morning and that there had been four men, possibly five, in a two-toned Chevrolet belonging to the young Blanton. I had been told about the car and shown a picture of it by FBI agents during the 1960s investigation. I told him that most of what I knew or believed I knew was from knowing Robert, his history of violence, and statements he had made to me.

(9TC)

INMATE STATIONARY FOR THE USE OF HOLMAN PRISON AND THE KILBY CORRECTIONS FACILITY

Feb. 20th 1978

Rev. Preacher.
  16th. Street Babtist Church
  16th Street 6th ave. North
  Birmingham ala.

Items permissible via mail service; Will consist of U.S. Money orders, solid color socks, white underwear, white handkerchiefs (all must be made of cotton) and black or tan shoes.

Items not allowed brought or sent into the institution; Food or drinks of any desription, electric appliances of any kind, tobacco, matches and cigarettes.

Money may be deposited for inmate with Officer in charge on visiting days.

Kneel

Dear Pastor Read this to your Congogation I Would
on my Mothers Grave Pray to you I've never homed
any thing Killed anybody or Bin in Tommy
Blanton's Car in my Life So help me God
Bill Bapley sent His Investagators to Detroit To get
that Woman to Come Down here and sware lies on me
He Flew Up there in a national Guard Plane Showed
Her my Picture and the Picture of Tommy Blanton's
Car got Her to Sware I Was in His Car With Door open
and She could idivefy me over 20 feet away By Dome
Light Paid Her 100 000 Dollars the Crazy Woman
Was'nt Crazy She Was a C.I.a. member
my Wife's niece aint nothing the Methodist don't
ordain or Licen Women to Preach they Coached Her
on What to Say and Paid Her When it comes to the
showdown. there Will Be 5 C.I.a. members / Police
or more Rev. Bapley is Just after the Colored
Votes I hope a Pray the Colored People have got
Better Since than to Vote for Him.
                        Yours Truly.
            R. E. Chambliss.
        Kilby Correctional Center Fac
          Rt 5 Box 125.
              Montgomery ala
                        36109

Robert Chambliss wrote this letter from his prison cell to the congregation of Sixteenth Street Baptist Church on February 20, 1978.

The conviction of Chambliss and his sentence of life imprisonment did bring a measure of accomplishment and justice. But the parents of the four young ladies and many other people questioned why it took so long for the wheels of justice to turn in this particular case when so many of the facts were known in 1963. Cynthia Wesley's father said the FBI had told him that they knew it was Robert Chambliss from the beginning. Carole Robertson's mother said that the trial should have come years before, and it was only Attorney General Bill Baxley's singular interest in the case that had brought Chambliss to justice in 1977.

Justice moves slowly in Alabama, and the single prosecution of only one man, Chambliss, for the death of only one of the four young ladies, Denise McNair, was a strategy devised by Mr. Baxley to ensure Chambliss's conviction. In a letter Chambliss wrote from prison to Sixteenth Street Baptist Church on February 20, 1978, he contended that he was not responsible for the bombing. Although he maintained his innocence until his death in prison in 1985, others knew that Chambliss was a ruthless man who hated blacks and rejected integration. They also knew that Chambliss did not act alone—he had help in planning the bombing of Sixteenth Street Baptist Church and placing the sticks of dynamite under the outside stairs. Two of Chambliss's probable accomplices named by Elizabeth Cobbs during the trial were later found dead— Troy Ingram in an automobile and John Wesley Hall in bed in Florida.

After several years of trying to bring others involved in the bombing to justice, the investigation into the Sixteenth Street Baptist Church bombing ground to a halt. After Attorney General Bill Baxley left office, no one picked up his lead and the case was dropped. Several times since 1977, including as recently as 1997, rumors have circulated that the case would be reopened.

Although the investigation into the bombing and the trial of Robert Chambliss stand out as dominant events in the history of Sixteenth Street Baptist Church during the mid to late seventies, the church's congregation continued its ongoing mission of witness and service to the community, still under the Reverend Crutcher's leadership. His pastorate remained challenged, however, and some members of the congregation once again called for his resignation at a quarterly conference held on Wednesday, October 24, 1979. As the meeting progressed and the congregation reached the point on the agenda when the Reverend Crutcher's contract was to be reviewed, one of the church's Trustees made a motion that the pastor submit his resignation within thirty days. The minutes of the conference record that "In the event that he does not resign in this period of time, the church will take necessary steps to cancel his contract and declare the pulpit

Birmingham Mayor Dr. Richard Arrington Jr.

vacant. This voting will be done by secret ballot." Approximately 130 people in attendance at the October 24th meeting voted to ask the Reverend Crutcher to resign.

While the Reverend Crutcher was facing a congregation attempting to oust him, the City of Birmingham was bracing itself for major political change. In 1979 Dr Richard Arrington Jr., Ph.D., a biology professor and dean at Miles College and a city council member, was elected Birmingham's first black mayor. Dr. Arrington was born in Sumter County, and his family later moved to Fairfield, near Birmingham, where his father worked in the steel mills. A graduate of Miles College, Arrington had firsthand knowledge of the city's problems and creatively explored new ways of addressing them. The major obstacle facing the new mayor, and the reason Arrington had been elected, was the fierce police brutality against blacks. Like the Reverend Crutcher, Mayor Arrington faced strong opposition, but Arrington's opposition came from both whites and blacks.

In 1980 Sixteenth Street Baptist Church received the special honor of being one of only two churches placed that year on the National Register of Historic Places by the National Trust for Historic Preservation. That listing recognizes the achievements of black architect Wallace Rayfield and black contractor Thomas C. Windham, and it also ensures that the architectural integrity of the facility can not be changed. Having their church listed as a historic place also helped the Sixteenth Street Baptist Church congregation recognize the uniqueness of their facility and ministry.

Former Alabama Governor, the Honorable Jim Folsom, wrote that "as a landmark identified with social change and reconciliation, this institution continues a legacy of more than one hundred twenty years." Mr. Rodney Slater, Secretary of the U.S. Department of Transportation, wrote that Sixteenth Street Baptist Church "serves as a sacred shrine to those who have sacrificially given their lives and subsequently made the paths of other African Americans brighter." The insights that these people shared were anchored in past events such as the use of Sixteenth Street Baptist Church as a meeting place for planning the Civil Rights Movement, the starting site of mass demonstrations in downtown Birmingham, and the September 1963 bombing. Slowly emerging from the pieces of history was the continuation of Sixteenth Street Baptist Church's role in Birmingham as a community church.

At the same time the church was receiving special recognition from external sources, internal strife was severely limiting its ability to do much for itself. As the problems between the Reverend Crutcher and the congregation escalated, the congregation of Sixteenth Street Baptist Church began a dysfunctional pattern that it would repeat with two future pastors.

In 1981 the congregation made a major financial commitment to repair the 1912 two-manual Pilcher Pipe Organ. Howard Best, the organ restorer, determined the repairs would cost $33,000 and he guaranteed that the work would be completed within six months from the date the contract was signed. The congregation signed the contract with Best in August 1981 and made an initial payment toward the total repair cost. The repairs were to be complete in time for Easter 1982.

The restoration of the pipe organ gives an example of what the members of Sixteenth Street Baptist Church can do when it focuses on a noble goal. Despite the reality that the congregation was suffering financially, the members were able over several months to raise thousands of dollars toward the final repair bill. By July 20, 1981, they had raised $11,000. As of October 11, they had raised $6,000 more, for a total of $17,000. By December 16, only $13,000 more remained to be raised, and Best reported to the congregation that the organ would be ready by March 1982. But by April 14, 1982, only a total of $24,000 had been raised and the organ had not been returned. By December 1982, only 75 percent of the organ restoration was completed, and the congregation had made only two payments of $8,000 each. The most diligent efforts of the church's members seemed difficult to maximize, and Best continued to disappoint them by not returning the restored organ within the contracted time frame.

In addition to facing the unresolved issues about the repair of the organ in 1982, the congregation of Sixteenth Street Baptist Church also faced many unresolved issues about the pastorate of the Reverend Crutcher. At a meeting held April 14, 1982, various church members complained about a number of things regarding the Reverend Crutcher. Some members complained that the worship services were unusually long and suggested the need to control the worship services so they would end on time, preferably within one hour. Other members alleged that the Reverend Crutcher did not make himself accessible to the church membership and that he had poor relationships with many church members, especially the Deacons. Someone else complained that there was too much idle talk in the pulpit and that the pulpit was being used as a battleground. One of the Trustees reported that he had been stopped by the police and accused of threatening and intimidating the Reverend Crutcher. One of the Deacons claimed that the Reverend Crutcher had intimidated him for not standing firm on an issue. When it became apparent that everything being said at the meeting was leading to a major "fight," Mrs. Willie S. Goodson made a motion for adjournment, and it was seconded.

A month later, in a special called meeting on May 19, 1982, ninety-two church members voted to vacate the pulpit, with only five members voting against the motion. A total of only ninety-seven members voting on such a major decision seems to suggest that the majority of the church's membership did not take issues facing the church seriously. Several times in its history the congregation of Sixteenth Street Baptist Church had displayed this same disinterested attitude toward important decisions, something that hurt the ministry of the church.

The church had also suffered grievously in many ways because some members refused to separate personality issues from principles. Often when members disagreed with the pastoral leadership, attendance would drop. People would become inactive or even join other churches. There would be little growth in membership (only seven new members joined in 1982, two of them by reinstatement), and the finances necessary to operate the church would dramatically decrease. Church members pointed fingers at each other for causing the problems.

Ironically, in attempting to remove the Reverend Crutcher in 1982 the congregation once again involved the Jefferson County court system, creating another embarrassing public spectacle for the congregation of Sixteenth Street Baptist Church. When some church members locked the doors of the church to prevent certain segments of the congregation from entering the building, the members who were locked out worshiped on the church steps.

The Birmingham media covered and reported it all. Elaine Witt, a reporter for the *Birmingham Post-Herald*, reported that the church was "traumatized" by the firing of a pastor that led to a court battle and a sharp drop in membership.

At a congregational conference on Sunday, December 19, 1982, the Reverend Crutcher read a letter of resignation. He stated that the Holy Spirit had spoken to him and given him the understanding to preach elsewhere, which he did and continues to do. At the end of 1982 the congregation of Sixteenth Street Baptist Church did not have a pastor—and its historic organ still had not been repaired.

At the church conference held July 13, 1983, the Pulpit Committee established the criteria it would use for selecting the next pastor of Sixteenth Street Baptist Church.

1. Is a believer and good Christian with a good background
2. Education: College graduate—Bachelor's degree and preferably Divinity Training
3. Age: 35-55 (can be flexible)
4. Experience: Spiritual speaker—Pastoral Experience
5. Good Health
6. A pastor to meet the needs of the church. Full-time minister. No divided time
7. Marital Status: If not married, give consideration. Debatable: Church can decide

Someone asked that item No. 6 be eliminated, and the members attending the meeting agreed. In a separate meeting of the Pulpit Committee, the criteria were further detailed.

A. *Is a Believer and good Christian—Good Background*
1. Acceptance of the Ten Commandments as a pattern for Christian living
2. Belief that salvation of sinners comes from one's belief in Christ's virgin birth, His blood shed by death on the Cross for remission of sins, and His Resurrection from the dead after three days
3. Belief in Baptist doctrine e.g. baptism by immersion as a symbol of the new Christian's burial of his sins
4. References for good background: 1 Timothy 3:2, 3, 4, 5, 6, 7; King James Version; Hiscox p. 61, Note 1; Titus 1:5-12, King James Version; Hiscox

Standard Baptist Manual p. 48, 2nd paragraph; Living Bible 1 Timothy 3:1-5; Living Bible Titus 1:5-12

B. *Education*

1. College Graduate

2. Bachelor's degree and preferably Divinity Training

C. *Age: 35-55*—Can be flexible—give or take

D. *Experience*

1. Pastoral Experience—Minimum of two years pastoral experience—Hiscox p. 61, Note 2. 1 Timothy 3:6

E. *Good Health*—One who is able to take care of normal pastoral duties and responsibilities Hiscox p. 48, first paragraph

F. *The Pastor can be given the opportunity with an outside occupation as long as it does not conflict with the duties and obligations to Sixteenth Street Church*

G. *Marital Status*

1. If not married, give consideration

2. Debatable—Church could decide

   1 Corinthian[s] 7:1, 2, 5-9 King James Version

   1 Corinthian[s] 7:1, 2, 6-9 Living Bible

The Pulpit Committee selected the Rev. Abraham L. Good from a group that included three other ministers, and on November 16, 1983, the congregation voted to call the Reverend Good to be pastor of Sixteenth Street Baptist Church. The congregation drafted an agreement between the church and the Reverend Good that included twelve points, a legal document that would hopefully avoid the problems the congregation had faced in dismissing the Reverend Crutcher.

Calling the Reverend Good fulfilled the congregation's urgent need to return to business as usual. It also fulfilled the congregation's desire to quickly replace the Reverend Crutcher and begin repairing the church's blemished public image.

The Reverend Good was born in Chattanooga, Tennessee, and educated in the city's public schools. He received training for the ministry at Moody Bible Institute in Chicago and Zion Bible College in Chattanooga. Before coming to Sixteenth Street Baptist Church, the Reverend Good served churches in Tennessee.

In the first days of his pastorate at Sixteenth Street Baptist Church, the Reverend Good had to contend with several leftover issues, including the uncompleted repairs of the pipe organ and the need for repairs on the facility. The Trustees had received a bid from a local construction company for $42,000 to repair the roof of the sanctuary building, replace wood damaged by termites, paint certain areas of the building, and do some work in the administrative (office) building. Under the Reverend Good's leadership the congregation sued Howard Best for failing to return the organ to the church by the contract deadline, and the organ was eventually placed back in service. Church membership increased under the Reverend Good's pastorate in 1984, with thirty-six persons joining the congregation.

The Rev. Abraham L. Good, Pastor 1983–1985. Photograph copyright, The Birmingham News, 1997. All rights reserved. Reprinted with permission.

Despite the membership growth, the return of the repaired organ, completion of some of the much-needed repair work, and other positive results achieved under the Reverend Good's leadership, the congregation continued their pattern of displaying negative characteristics that had caused problems in previous pastoral administrations. The resignations/retirements of several key lay leaders, including the treasurer, assistant treasurer, and chairman of the Finance Committee, indicated that something serious was amiss. Four months later at a church conference that was described as "great confusion," the Reverend Good dictated a sentence to the clerk, Myrtle C. Whetstone, offering his resignation. When the Reverend Good resigned on April 17, 1985, associate minister James L. Lowe Jr. and several families left and formed the core congregation of a new church named the Guiding Light Church, a ministry that continues to thrive.

At the same time the congregation of Sixteenth Street Baptist Church was experiencing tumultuous change and the loss of members, Birmingham was also experiencing tumultuous change as well as the continuing loss of white citizens to the suburbs south and east of the city limits. For the first time in Birmingham's history, blacks became the majority population, with a total of 158,000 blacks to 125,000 whites. Other racial groups also lived in Birmingham, but their numbers were small. The congregation of Sixteenth Street Baptist Church needed to focus on their ministry both their members and to the community at this turning point in Birmingham's development, and they would need a strong leader to guide their ministry. Once again, however, the congregation followed its dysfunctional pattern of choosing a new pastor.

It is difficult to believe that people do not learn from previous mistakes or do not stop long enough to assess and ask the simple question, "What happened?" Perhaps the congregation of Sixteenth Street Baptist Church did not stop long enough after the traumatic dismissal of the Reverend Crutcher to seek God's guidance in selecting a new pastor—perhaps they should have gone through a serious evaluation of the church's ministry before they called the Reverend Good. Such an evaluation would have been helpful in determining the kind of leadership that would have been appropriate for the congregation. Furthermore, an evaluation of the membership would have indicated problems with the congregation that should have been addressed and solved before hiring a new pastor.

Many churches go several years before selecting the next pastor to fill a vacancy. The interim not only allows time for the congregation to evaluate their situation, but it also gives the congregation time to heal, especially when the former pastorate may have been complicated and troublesome.

The members of Sixteenth Street Baptist Church realized that they needed to do something along the lines of an evaluation, and they convened a Task Force whose mission was to determine the reasons for the decrease in membership. The Task Force would ask 130 members a series of questions and record their responses. The responses would be tabulated and summarized in a report that would be distributed at a congregational meeting.

The members present at the October 16, 1985, church conference approved a motion to meet three weeks later and fully discuss the report prepared by the Task Force. The goal of the meeting would be for the congregation to approve the report and vote to implement all or some of the Task Force's recommendations. The congregation expected the Deacons and Trustees, the lay leadership of the church, to address and take action on the Task Force's recommendations.

At a special called congregational conference on November 6, 1985, the Task Force gave its report, which revealed that the church had an active membership of 150 members, only 100 of the members contributed financially to the operating expenses, and approximately 75 people attended Sunday worship services. The Task Force report included recommendations that were approved by the church members who were present. One of the recommendations was that the Deacon and Trustee Boards follow a three-year rotation schedule. The Deacons and Trustees attending the meeting agreed and said they would present the details for establishing the rotation schedule at a subsequent meeting.

The November 6th meeting ended with the Task Force being invited to present suggestions for implementing the approved recommendations at the regular December congregational conference. At the congregational conference on December 11, 1985, a church member made a motion that the Task Force's recommendations be implemented. The motion failed, and the Task Force was never heard of again.

Forming the Task Force was a good initiative and the responses to the questionnaire identified core problems, but the lay leadership never fully implemented the Task Force's recommendations. In essence, the congregation of Sixteenth Street Baptist Church didn't complete a serious evaluation, something that might have helped them avoid repeating the devastating, embarrassing mistakes they had made in the past. The congregation had not taken the time to do an evaluation or heal before they had hired the Reverend Good—nor did they take the time before they hired their next pastor. As could be expected, the next pastorate would yield similar disastrous results.

During the time the church was without a pastor after the Reverend Good resigned, church membership continued to decline as members moved to other churches or simply stopped coming to Sixteenth Street Baptist Church. The decline in membership may have prompted the congregation to disband the Pulpit Committee formed immediately after the Reverend Good's resignation and form a new one. The decline in membership may also have prompted the new Pulpit Committee to act hastily to fill the vacancy.

The original Pulpit Committee had considered several persons for the pastorate, including a minister who was licensed by Sixteenth Street Baptist Church. On February 5, 1986, the new Pulpit Committee members reported that they had investigated five out-of-state candidates and had contacted four of them to see if they were still interested in the position. Members of the Pulpit Committee visited two of the four final candidates in the churches they were serving. On the recommendation of the Pulpit Committee, the congregation voted at a meeting held on May 21, 1986, to call the Rev. James E. Young to become the next pastor of Sixteenth Street Baptist Church.

At the time he was called, the Reverend Young was serving a church in Tennessee. When he arrived in Birmingham, he found, as his predecessors had, that there were many leftover issues that required his immediate attention. A new Director of Music had to be hired. The pipe organ had not been repaired properly. The steps of the sanctuary building needed major repair work. Several parts of the facility needed repainting. The public address system in the sanctuary needed to be replaced. The electrical system in the sanctuary needed a new transformer. A feasibility study needed to be done to evaluate the possibility of adding an elevator.

Those issues were more than enough to keep the new pastor busy, and the Reverend Young needed the congregation's support in resolving them. Again, however, the congregation of Sixteenth Street Baptist Church continued its pattern of meetings filled with insulting words spoken by one member against another and by some members against the pastor. It became obvious early in his pastorate that the Reverend Young and the congregation would experience a time of little progress.

Under the Reverend Young's leadership the congregation settled with the organ restorer for $3,000 and contracted with a consultant to determine the worth the restorer's work. The consultant reported that the repair work was totally inadequate. Although playable, the organ would not be fully operational until years later.

At the October 14, 1987, congregation conference, one church member abruptly motioned that the pulpit be vacated. Although the other church members present ruled the motion invalid, the stage was set for the Reverend Young's demise as pastor of Sixteenth Street Baptist Church.

The Rev. Abraham L. Good (third from right), Pastor 1983-1985

At a congregational conference a year later on October 12, 1988, another motion was made to declare the pulpit vacant, and a standing vote of the church members present passed the motion. At this point, the Reverend Young left the meeting.

The Reverend Young had already received several letters on church stationery outlining complaints against him, including his leadership, sermon topics, and public attacks against members of the church from the pulpit. Over the years members of the Sixteenth Street Baptist Church and even citizens of Birmingham have spoken negatively about the pastorate of the Reverend Young and its detriment to the church. A tenure of only fifteen months says that the relationship between the Reverend Young and the congregation was not amicable. As with his two immediate predecessors, the differences between the congregation and the Reverend Young turned everyone's focus away from the important vision of the ministry of Sixteenth Street Baptist Church. The differences between the pastor and the congregation could not be resolved, and in 1988 the Reverend Young returned to his native state of Tennessee.

The Rev. Dr. Christopher M. Hamlin speaking from the steps of Sixteenth Street Baptist Church during a community demonstration held in April 1992 to protest a rally of Ku Klux Klan members and Skinheads in Birmingham's Linn Park

PUTTING THE PIECES BACK TOGETHER

• • • • • •

At the April 12, 1989, church conference, the congregation established a Pulpit Committee and named Arthur Means Jr. as chairperson. After several months of planning and screening applications, the Pulpit Committee recommended on November 29, 1989 that I, Christopher M. Hamlin, be called to become pastor of Sixteenth Street Baptist Church.

I accepted the call and became the sixteenth pastor of Sixteenth Street Baptist Church on January 7, 1990. When I assumed the pastorate the church had a worshiping community of approximately seventy-five people. I soon realized that the congregation was wearied from years of poor decisions on the part of both pastoral and lay leadership.

I have concluded after years of studying the personalities of the congregation and the role of the church in the community that in 1990 Sixteenth Street Baptist Church was dying and in need of internal reconciliation. During the first two years of my ministry I concentrated on rebuilding relationships, building new ones, and developing trust between the pastoral and lay leadership of the church and the church members as well as trust between each of us as individuals. In the more than seven years I have served Sixteenth Street Baptist Church, I have witnessed the power of God in transforming the lives of people who love their church and are concerned about their faith. I welcomed the transformations and realize how difficult it was for many of the church members.

In addition to taking immediate steps to reduce ongoing internal strife and heal wounded relationships, I also quickly undertook rebuilding of the membership of Sixteenth Street Baptist Church, preserving the historic facility, and developing programs to benefit both members and nonmembers. For a number of years the congregation had neglected the important tasks of ministry and maintenance. Although several organizations continued to use our facility and visitors continued to tour it, both of these community

State of Alabama

The Sixteenth Street Baptist Church

The National Register of Historic Places
United States Department of the Interior

September 17, 1980

Alabama Historical Commission

Kermit Johnson

ministries needed to be better defined. Unfortunately the congregation had stopped heeding the mandate for which Sixteenth Street Baptist Church had been established in 1873—to be a congregational church that reached out into the community.

After receiving the honor of having Sixteenth Street Baptist Church placed on the National Register by the National Trust for Historic Preservation in 1980, the congregation made several attempts to renovate the sanctuary building. Unfortunately the church members did not develop a substantial strategy or fundraising plans to underwrite such a costly endeavor. Prior to my arrival as pastor of the church, the General Missionary Society and other church members gave funds to renovate the office building and some minor repairs were made, but none of the efforts to restore the sanctuary were completed.

I believe that as a congregation we must protect and preserve our historic sacred site at all costs. As Diane Cohen and A. Robert Jaeger, of Partners for Sacred Places, wrote in "Affirming Our Collective Stake in Safeguarding Sacred Places," published in the February/March 1995 issue of *Historic Preservation News*, "If we allow America's historic religious properties to decline and disappear, we will lose much more than the rich, soulful story they tell. We will lose those rare, affordable, welcoming places that are generating new energies and resources to meet the larger challenges faced by America's communities."

By the time I arrived in Birmingham, the city had already made the commitment of building a facility devoted to highlighting Birmingham's involvement in the Civil Rights Movement. The city had chosen a property across the street from Sixteenth Street Baptist Church as the site for the new building, and as soon as I realized the magnitude of the city's project, I met with Mayor Richard Arrington Jr. to get a better understanding of the impact of this project on our church. I was fascinated to hear Mayor Arrington's dreams of creating the world's premier center for civil rights in the world and using it as a vehicle to improve race relations in our metropolitan community. I knew that we at Sixteenth Street Baptist Church had to pursue the possibility of working with Mayor Arrington and the City of Birmingham in this momentous opportunity.

In 1992 I recommended that the congregation assess the possibility of launching a capital campaign to raise money to preserve and restore the Sixteenth

Birmingham Civil Rights Institute under construction in 1992

Street Baptist Church building to its 1911 grandeur. The congregation agreed with the assessment, and we began a $2.5 million capital campaign. Since then we have raised or have commitments for more than $1.1 million toward this project. Perhaps equally as important as the success of our capital campaign is the renewed level of energy, cooperation, and enthusiasm we feel as a congregation.

As we pursue ways of making sure that our facility remains a vibrant part of Birmingham's historic landscape, we must be careful to maintain the original intent of the founding members of Sixteenth Street Baptist Church. They desired a facility that would be at the center of their community, and their vision was to create an open-door church that would serve the needs of those so readily denied access to other public facilities. The leadership and current membership of Sixteenth Street Baptist Church are committed to putting the pieces back together and then maintaining our historic facility as a center of ministry for all peoples.

The congregation that I found hopeless in 1990 has found hope in experiencing a rebirth, reconciling internal differences, and reclaiming a 125-year-old heritage. Our membership has grown and continues to grow. We have developed new programs and ministries that are making a difference in the lives of people in our metropolitan community and beyond. We have a calmer demeanor that is transforming every aspect of our ministry.

After careful analysis and discussions with various members of our congregation, I have concluded that Sixteenth Street Baptist Church is more than a church in the generic sense of the word. The vital role we have played in the history of the City of Birmingham and the United States has dictated that we expand the vision our founders had 125 years ago of serving our immediate community.

Our Sixteenth Street Baptist Church building stands as a powerful symbol of a courageous spirit that has helped make every American—as well people from around the world—more truly free. Our historic facility serves as a resource center for information about the Civil Rights Movement. People from around the globe make pilgrimages to our facility to visit the site where four young ladies lost their lives on Sunday morning, September 15, 1963.

More than 90,000 people visit Sixteenth Street Baptist Church each year to tour the facility and take part in group events. These local and world citizens

First Lady Hillary Rodham Clinton came to Sixteenth Street Baptist Church for a rally in 1992.

come seeking understanding and answers to probing questions. Our congregation has made a commitment to respond to all our visitors by being present in every way we can. Mrs. Marvine Bradford, one of our members, says that our facility "has been many things to many people—a church, a place for leaders to teach, a place to embrace ethnic culture, a place to also receive inspiration from those who come together for the good of ALL people."

As a 1,600-seat facility, our building continues its historic role as a community meeting place. We host a variety of social, cultural, and political events important to the life of our city and nation. During the segregation era, Sixteenth Street Baptist Church served as a mini-civic center for Birmingham's African American community, and many outstanding national African Americans attended events here during the first half of this century.

During the last five years the Honorable Andrew Young, the Rev. Jesse Jackson, Hillary Rodham Clinton, Janet Reno, Julian Bond, Ossie Davis, Dr. Mae Jemison, Dr. Ben Carson, Dr. Margaret Walker Alexander, and Dr. Clarissa Penkola Estes have been among the many nationally and internationally known leaders to speak at events held at Sixteenth Street Baptist Church. Since 1993 our congregation has hosted a tribute to Thurgood Marshall, National Conference of Christians and Jews conferences, workshops

Janie Gaines, sister of Addie Mae Collins, the Rev. Dr. Christopher M. Hamlin, and Attorney General Janet Reno at Sixteenth Street Baptist Church on January 15, 1997

The Reverend Hamlin, the Reverend Shuttlesworth, Mayor Richard Arrington Jr., and the Honorable Andrew Young during the dedication service for the Birmingham Civil Rights Institute on November 15, 1992

and events focusing on AIDS, religious denominational events, an Anti-Death Penalty Conference, and a major address by AIDS advocate Mary Fisher.

We have also hosted many music events, including Wynton Marsalis and his Septet featuring "In This House, On This Morning," a piece Marsalis wrote to be played in houses of worship and performed on his national tour. We welcomed a choir competition with actor and musician Jester Hairston as the clinician. Choral groups from Morehouse Colege, Rust College, Talladega College, Alabama A&M University, Alabama State University, and Samford University have performed in our sanctuary. We also hosted the Citadel Gospel Choir in concert.

During a recent Birmingham Festival of the Arts program, we were fortunate to have a glee club from Wales visit our facility. The glee club's members were anxious to see the "Wales Window for Alabama," the window that the children of Cardiff, Wales, paid for by collecting pennies and that was designed by Welsh stained-glass artist John Petts to replace a window broken in the 1963 bomb explosion. The singers gave an impromptu concert in the sanctuary during their visit, a very emotional event for us as well as the singers.

Sixteenth Street Baptist Church continues to serve as a cultural and human rights crossroads. In 1994 we hosted one of the regional conferences on

A glee club from Wales gave an improptu performance in the sanctuary after seeing the Wales Window for Alabama, designed by Welsh stained-glass artist John Petts.

racism and human rights sponsored by the National and World Council of Churches. The regional office of the National Conference of Christians and Jews frequently brings students to Sixteenth Street Baptist Church to discuss prejudice reduction and elimination. We joined with the City of Birmingham in welcoming hundreds of thousands of people to the international soccer matches held here as part of the 1996 Summer Olympic Games hosted by Atlanta.

Sixteenth Street Baptist Church heartily embraces the range of roles in our mission. From our founding to our current ministry, we open our doors to the world in willingness to be light for the world's darkness.

Recently we called on consultant Robert Wiltshire to help us clarify the ministry of Sixteenth Street Baptist Church. We have determined that we have three levels of service:

1) *To advance the Gospel.*

As a Christian institution located in Birmingham since 1873, Sixteenth Street Baptist Church has remained mindful of God's injunction to the Hebrew prophet Isaiah (Isaiah 61:1-3a) "to bring good tidings to the afflicted, to bind up the brokenhearted, to proclaim liberty to the captives and opening of the prison to those who are bound . . . to comfort all who mourn . . . to give them a garland instead of ashes, the oil of gladness instead of mourning, the mantle of praise instead of a faint spirit."

During the segregation era our church had a membership of 900 or more. Urban renewal practices over the past thirty years have demolished the residential neighborhood surrounding our facility and prompted a corresponding decline in membership. Local demographic shifts plus ministerial leadership issues combined to further reduce to 200 or less at the end of the 1980s. Our congregation is now experiencing a resurgence in membership, program, and facilities.

2) *To serve the community.*

Sixteenth Street Baptist Church continues to play a vital role in the Birmingham community. Our function as a host for community activities is especially notable. Along with numerous other events, we host an annual interpretive class for Leadership Birmingham, an organization that brings together approximately forty-five community leaders for an eight-month evluative assessment of the metropolitan area.

Students from local schools made models of historic downtown buildings, including Sixteenth Street Baptist Church, for a Birmingham Historical Society's Preservation Week celebration.

As further affirmation of the value of our community service, the Birmingham Area Chamber of Commerce has listed Sixteenth Street Baptist Church as one of the thirty-two best things about the City of Birmingham.

Our historic facility serves as a cornerstone for the recently developed Birmingham Civil Rights District. The Birmingham Historical Society has included Sixteenth Street Baptist Church in its effort to develop an industrial heritage district of the South's important iron and steel center from the Civil War through World War II. In this context Sixteenth Street symbolizes the indispensable role of African American labor in Birmingham's industrial development.

3) To witness to the ends of the earth.

In fall 1992 Birmingham's Civil Rights Institute opened its doors across the street from Sixteenth Street Baptist Church. This state-of-the-art museum and teaching facility depicts historical events from the days of racial separation to present-day racial progress. Sixteenth Street Baptist Church serves as the unofficial auditorium for major events sponsored by the Institute.

EAST ELEVATION

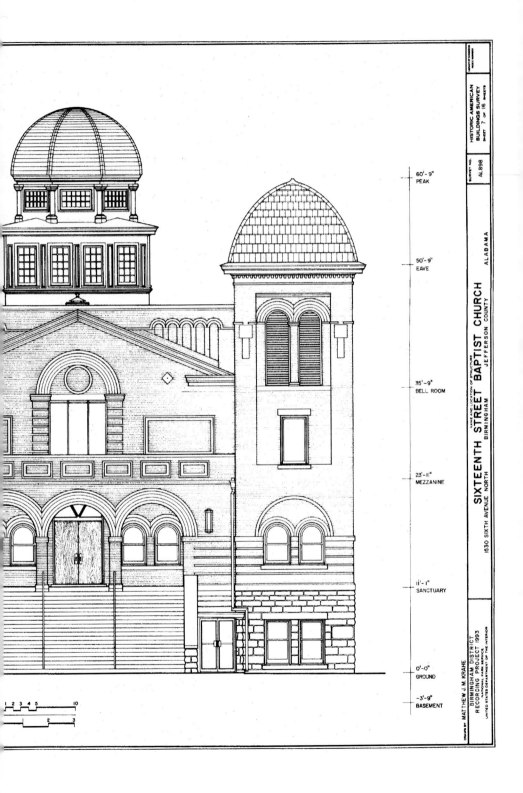

60' - 9"
PEAK

50' - 9"
EAVE

35' - 9"
BELL ROOM

23' - 11"
MEZZANINE

11' - 1"
SANCTUARY

0' - 0"
GROUND

-3' - 9"
BASEMENT

1 2 3 4 5   10

2   3

DRAWN BY MATTHEW J. M. KRAHE

BIRMINGHAM DISTRICT
RECORDING PROJECT 1993
NATIONAL PARK SERVICE
UNITED STATES DEPARTMENT OF THE INTERIOR

SIXTEENTH STREET BAPTIST CHURCH
1530 SIXTH AVENUE NORTH   BIRMINGHAM   JEFFERSON COUNTY   ALABAMA

NAME AND LOCATION OF STRUCTURE

SURVEY NO.
AL 898

HISTORIC AMERICAN
BUILDINGS SURVEY
SHEET 7 OF 16 SHEETS

GROUP OF SHEETS
INDEX NUMBER

During this past year, visitor and pilgrimage traffic at Sixteenth Street Baptist Church has increased. People now come here from around the globe in remembrance of the courage of marchers who assembled in our historic facility and followed Dr. King and the Reverend Shuttlesworth into the resistance of police dogs and fire hoses that blocked the path to integration and equality.

In 1993 the thirtieth anniversary of the September 15, 1963, bombing brought Sixteenth Street Baptist Church renewed national attention. Our congregation lived a tragedy that still reminds all of us of the naked truth of justice.

On July 9, 1997, local FBI agents and the Birmingham Police Department announced that they were officially reopening the investigation into 1963 bombing. Twelve months earlier investigators had begun reevaluating the files and suspects that were fingered during the original 1963 investigation as well as the files from the 1977 investigation and trial of Robert Chambliss. An interview of Bobby Frank Cherry, who lives outside Dallas, Texas, yielded another denial of his involvement in the 1963 bombing. Thomas E. Blanton Jr., who lives in Fultondale and has been questioned as part of the reopening of the investigation, also continues to deny his involvement. These men, along with Herman Cash, remain prime suspects from 1963. Bob Eddy, an investigator who worked with Bill Baxley in bringing Robert Chambliss to trial in 1977, emphasizes that the 1997 investigators are starting with the same suspects he and his fellow investigators questioned. "They were the same suspects in 1963 and '64," said Eddy in an interview with Carol Robinson for the August 31, 1997, issue of *The Birmingham News*. "It's still the same suspects. It's just as plain as it can be."

The special agent in charge of the Birmingham division of the FBI told *Birmingham News* reporter Carol Robinson that "it's a crime that has gone unsolved except for one local conviction, and it remains a sore part of American history that we would like to heal."

It's too early to know if new convictions will come from the current investigation of a crime that is now thirty-five years old. Because Sunday, September 15, 1963, was such a dismal day in the history of Sixteenth Street Baptist Church, additional convictions of those who plotted and planted a bomb that destroyed four innocent lives, injured twenty-two others, caused substantial damage to our facility, and forever changed the ministry of our church would help us reaffirm our mission of being a voice crying against systemic injustice in our world. The completion of this case would allow Sixteenth Street Baptist Church to seal a broken piece of our stained glass.

LETTING THE LIGHT SHINE

● ● ● ● ● ●

Much has been written, especially from a secular point of view, about the value of remembering and preserving significant historical events by establishing memorials. The U.S. Department of Interior has been instrumental in initiating, through the National Trust for Historic Preservation and other agencies, concern for secular buildings and properties that have played a significant role in defining America. In recent years religious-based groups have begun requesting that secular institutions also recognize the significance of sacred sites. Sacred as well as secular sites, including memorials and public art projects, across the United States remind us of various events and personalities that helped shape our national and global community.

Historic memorials, both secular and sacred, can be found in designated parks, on plazas of government buildings, in private-sector facilities, schools, libraries, museums, homes, houses of worship, and religious education buildings. They represent a vast collection of interpretations of events and contributions

Dwayne Coleman's 1992 rendering of Sixteenth Street Baptist Church

made by individuals and groups. Without using words, many of them tell illuminating stories and reveal understandings about our nation and its people.

According to *Sacred Sites, Sacred Places*, "some sites that have religious significance may also assume historical or political importance." Many buildings and facilities are associated with social movements that redefined America. For African Americans there has always been an undeniable affinity between religious experience and political movement, especially the Civil Rights Movement.

In *We Have Been Believers: An African-American Systematic Theology*, theologian, educator, and author Dr. James H. Evans Jr. said that "it is not accidental that with the political reawakening of African Americans in the 1960s there was also a spiritual reawakening."

The spiritual reawakening of the sixties demanded that we tell our story and demand others to see it, hear it, and understand it. Today Sixteenth Street Baptist Church continues "to tell our story" in words and deeds.

Our congregation has now grown to more than 500 active members. The majority of our members are professionals working in the fields of medicine,

Sixteenth Street Baptist Church Deacons and Deaconesses with the Reverend Hamlin in 1993

education, social services, law, and labor. Most of our church families own their homes, and many live in the suburbs of the City of Birmingham that are slowly becoming more ethnically diverse. Most of our members have received degrees beyond four years of college, and the majority of those people attended historically black institutions of higher learning, including Talladega College, Alabama State University, Alabama A&M University, Miles College, Morehouse College, Spelman College, and Clark Atlanta University. Several of our members attended the University of Alabama at Birmingham, the University of Alabama, Samford University, and Birmingham-Southern College for their undergraduate or graduate degrees.

We continue to be affiliated with denominational entities and support several auxiliaries and organizations within the church to meet the needs of our congregation. We recently began a mentoring program with one of our correctional facilities. Our members are mentoring fourteen young people with hope of making a difference in their lives.

Our outreach ministries include a fellowship meal for homeless people who reside in the city center, voice and instrumental lessons for the congregation and community, a clothing closet, and benevolent emergency aid. We continue to work with Greater Birmingham Ministries, United Way of Central Alabama, Operation New Birmingham, and other agencies to make positive differences in our community.

We have formed partnerships with the Greater Birmingham Convention and Visitors Bureau, Landmark Tours, Onyx Agency, the Birmingham Civil Rights Institute, the Alabama Jazz Hall of Fame, and other organizations to welcome the world to Birmingham.

Our congregation's mission is to fulfill our three levels of service: to advance the Gospel, to serve the community, and to witness to the ends of the earth. We seek to serve as a catalyst of prophetic and priestly ministry to transform our city, state, nation, and world. As a memorial church, we are in a pivotal position to help. We are also strategically situated to be a voice denouncing systemic ills that degrade humanity.

Sixteenth Street Baptist Church will remain a living memorial and a point of reference because people still express interest in the events of the past. People want to know what happened here on Sunday, September 15, 1963, why it happened, and how our city became such a deplorable place to live.

In April 1992 Birmingham police officers protected marchers as they left Kelly Ingram Park to protest a rally of Ku Klux Klan members and Skinheads in Linn Park.

It is imperative that when people look behind the stained glass, they understand the forces that made Birmingham such a horrible place for blacks during the days of segregation. It is also imperative that as they look behind the stained glass they see a Birmingham that has been transformed because people were committed to change and made the supreme sacrifice to make it happen. Sixteenth Street Baptist Church will remain a strong advocate for transforming society, especially where anyone's personhood is violated and racism is real.

We stand in solidarity with everyone oppressed by systemic ills, and we are committed to finding ways to remind everyone that we can rise above ills that seek to destroy us. We are establishing a reconciliation center, a self-sustained entity of our church that will partner with people and groups sponsoring diversity training. The center will also welcome workshops and cultural events that will address the issue of race relations and the need to end racism in all communities. It will also provide space for think tank groups to gather and seek solutions to community problems.

The center will also allow us to better serve the more than 90,000 visitors and pilgrims that come to Sixteenth Street Baptist Church every

People gathered on the steps of Sixteenth Street Baptist Church during a demonstration against a rally of Ku Klux Klan members and Skinheads in April 1992.

year. As the visitors enter the center, they will be invited to hear the story of our church and the vital role it played in the Civil Rights Movement. We expect and hope that after visiting the Birmingham Civil Rights District people will understand why four young ladies lost their lives because of the hatred of those who refused to accept African Americans as human beings, sisters and brothers made in the image and likeness of God.

We will invite visitors to look behind their own "glass," the glass in their own lives, in their communities. We will provide materials for them to use, and we will serve as resources for activities they can do in their hometowns.

America has changed in the thirty-five years since the bomb exploded at Sixteenth Street Baptist Church. The ministry of our church has also changed since that pivotal event. We are now more committed than ever to effect social change in our city, state, nation, and world—wherever people suffer brutality inflicted because of differences.

The recent burning of more than fifty churches under suspicious circumstances reminds us of the crucial need for persons who are different from each other to find common ground and to become tolerant of each other. Recent events in Bosnia also remind us of our struggle for tolerance. Continued strained relations in Israel and the West Bank remind us of the tensions that exist when people find it difficult to live together. The recent bombing of Birmingham's New Woman All Women clinic, which tragically took the life of a police officer and critically injured one of the clinic's nurses, also reminds us that the journey toward civil rights for all people is not over.

The transformations in South Africa assure us that we are making progress on our journey toward civil rights for all. In Birmingham, transforming progress took place because the survival of the city depended upon it. Birmingham's Civil Rights story is so powerful because the events that happened at Sixteenth Street Baptist Church in 1963 changed every aspect of the city—from political leadership to economic development and residential patterns. In 1963 Birmingham's black citizens stated in clear tones that they would not tolerate injustice and inequality in any sphere of their lives.

Sixteenth Street Baptist Church understands itself to be a memorial church, and therefore a primary task of our ministry is to remind our membership as well as the larger community that the stones of this church tell a moving story of survival, salvation, and liberation. Memorial churches do not gain this status on their own—it is forced upon them by significant events that impact a particular community.

In this city of paradoxes, Sixteenth Street Baptist Church was born and bombed. Its birth changed the city and its bombing changed the world. The stones of our memorial church will forever stand as a symbol of God's deliverance. The stones of Sixteenth Street Baptist Church will remind people of what happened here in 1963 and why it must never happen again.

EPILOGUE

• • • • • •

*I*t is impossible to do justice to every individual who identified and claimed Sixteenth Street Baptist Church as their spiritual home. The names are too many and their contributions too great to list all of them in this book. I have simply tried to relate in some detail the significance of this powerful story against the backdrop of Birmingham's founding in 1871 and the emergence of an African American congregation determined to make its home in the city center.

The statue of Dr. Martin Luther King Jr. in Kelly Ingram Park faces Sixteenth Street Baptist Church.

There are many parallels between the congregation of Sixteenth Street Baptist Church and the congregations of other churches. Like us, the members of every congregation experience their own set of struggles that help define their church's identify and what its legacy will be.

It is important that every effort be made to earnestly see the light shining through the stained glass of Sixteenth Street Baptist Church. That light illuminates paths of truth and understanding. It banishes the darkness that attempts to nullify the yearning for freedom and hope. Such light has been the guiding force of our ministry. The members of our congregation are to be commended for struggling through difficult days and celebrating joyous moments so that Sixteenth Street Baptist Church might continue to be a strong symbol of God's presence in Birmingham and the world.

As we celebrate our 125th anniversary, I am grateful to be serving as pastor of Sixteenth Street Baptist Church. Our congregation's future is bright and strong. Our church will remain a beacon of hope, an anchoring place in the City of Birmingham and a landmark in the world. The tragic events of 1963 that put this congregation in the international spotlight will never be used inappropriately. We will continue to remind present and future generations of the pivotal events that took place in Birmingham and at Sixteenth Street Church.

Behind the stained glass of our church is a poignant story that must be told. The stained glass illuminates an avenue that leads behind the facade to the discovery of the true story of the ministry and service that Sixteenth Street Baptist Church has provided for 125 years and will continue to provide. Looking behind the stained glass gives a unique perspective and a glimpses of deep truths.

Since 1990 I have been blessed to help shape the story of Sixteenth Street Baptist Church. Behind the stained glass I have witnessed God's grace in the lives of people and God's care for our world. I am on an amazing journey, and I am grateful that it continues.

Rebirth • Reconcile • Reclaim
Sixteenth Street Baptist Church
1873 • 125th Anniversary • 1998
Celebrating One Hundred • and • Twenty-Five Years

RESOURCE MATERIALS

● ● ● ● ● ●

4 Little Girls. Produced by Spike Lee and Sam Pollard and directed by Spike Lee, documentary film, 1997.

Angels of Change. Produced by WTVM Channel 13, Birmingham, Alabama, videocassette.

Ansbro, John J. *Martin Luther King Jr.: The Making of a Mind*. Maryknoll, New York: Orbis Books, 1983.

Atkins, Leah Rawls, Wayne Flynt, William Warren Rogers, and Robert David Ward. *Alabama: The History of a Deep South State*. Tuscaloosa: The University of Alabama Press, 1994.

Bell, Geraldine Watts. "Death in the Morning," *Down Home* (Fall 1982).

Bennett, Lerone Jr. *Before the Mayflower: A History of the Negro in America 1619–1964* , rev. ed. Baltimore: Penguin Books, 1968.

Boatner, Mark M., III. *Landmarks of the American Revolution: A Guide to Locating and Knowing What Happened at the Sites of Independence*. Harrisburg: Stackpole Books, 1973.

Branch, Taylor. *Parting the Waters: America in the King Years, 1954–1963*. New York: Simon & Schuster, 1988.

Brown, Charles A. "W. A. Rayfield: Pioneer Black Architect of Birmingham, Ala." Birmingham, Alabama: Gray Printing Company, 1972.

Carmichael, David L., Jane Hubert, Brian Reeves, Audhild Schanche, ed. *Sacred Sites, Sacred Places*. New York: Routledge, 1994.

"Civil Rights Memorial: A Movement of the People." Montgomery: The Southern Poverty Law Center, 1995.

Cohen, Diane and A. Robert Jaeger. "Affirming Our Collective Stake in Safeguarding Sacred Places." *Historic Preservation News* (February/March 1995).

Evans, James H., Jr. *We Have Been Believers: An African-American Systematic Theology*. Minneapolis: Fortress Press, 1992.

Flynt, Wayne. "Leadership Patterns in Birmingham's History." Birmingham, Alabama: Leadership Birmingham, 1987.

Foner, Eric. *Reconstruction: 1863–1877.* New York: Harper & Row Publishers, 1988.

Garrow, David J. *Bearing the Cross: Martin Luther King, Jr. and the Southern Christian Leadership Conference.* New York: William Morrow and Company, Inc., 1986.

—————. *Birmingham, Alabama, 1956–1963: The Black Struggle for Civil Rights.* New York: Carlson Publishing Inc., 1989.

Journal of Negro History, vol. xiv (1929).

King, Martin Luther, Jr. *Letter From Birmingham Jail.* Philadelphia: American Friends Service Committee, 1963.

Leighton, George R. "Birmingham, Alabama: The City of Perpetual Promise," *Harper's Magazine.* vol. 175 (August 1937).

Macquarrie, John. *Principles in Theology,* 2nd ed. New York: Charles Scribner's Sons, 1977.

Mays, Benjamin E. *Disturbed About Man.* Richmond: John Knox Press, 1969.

Mays, Benjamin E. and Joseph W. Nicholson. *The Negro's Church.* New York: Arno Press, 1969 reprint of 1933 edition.

National Park Service, Historic American Buildings Survey. "Sixteenth Street Baptist Church" (HABS No. AL-898). Washington, D.C.: National Park Service, 1993.

Nelson, Hart M., Raytha L. Yokley, and Anne K. Nelson, ed. *The Black Church in America.* New York: Basic Books, Inc., Publishers, 1973.

Nunnelley, William A. *Bull Connor.* Tuscaloosa, Alabama: The University of Alabama Press, 1991.

Oates, Stephen B. *Let the Trumpet Sound: The Life of Martin Luther King, Jr.* New York: Harper & Row, 1982.

Owens, Reginald. "Where Tourism and Tears Cross Paths." *The Tennessean* (July 3, 1994).

Raboteau, Albert J. *Slave Religion: The "Invisible Institution" in the Antebellum South.* New York: Oxford University Press, 1978.

Ragan, Larry. "Contractor & 'Sportin' Man," *The Birmingham News* (February 22, 1992).

Robinson, Carol. "Church Bomb Probe More than a Rehash," *The Birmingham News* (August 31, 1997).

Rowan, Carl T. *South of Freedom*. New York: Alfred A. Knopf, 1954.

Sarda, Michel. *John Henry Waddell: The Art and the Artist*. Phoenix, Arizona: Bridgewood Press, 1996.

Shane, Thomas. "Where Hope Abounds, Lives Are Rebuilt." *The Newton Kansan*, 1995.

Sikora, Frank. *Until Justice Rolls Down: The Birmingham Church Bombing Case*. Tuscaloosa: The University of Alabama Press, 1991.

Smith, Alison.*Welsh Horizons*. London: British Broadcasting Corporation, 1992.

Smith, Petric J. and Elizabeth H. Cobbs. *Long Time Coming*. Birmingham: Crane Hill Publishers, 1994.

Sterling, Dorothy. *Tear Down the Walls! A History of the American Civil Rights Movement*. Garden City, New York: Doubleday, 1968.

"The 32 Best Things About Birmingham," *Birmingham*, vol. 32, no. 4 (April 1992).

Thurman, Howard W. *The Centering Moment*. Richmond: Friends United Press, 1969.

——————. *The Inward Journey*. Richmond: Friends United Press, 1971.

Whitherspoon, John DuBose. *Jefferson County and Birmingham, Alabama: Historical and Biographical*. Birmingham: Teeple & Smith, Publishers, 1887.

Witt, Elaine. "Church's Problems Don't Faze Pastor: Bombing, Court Fight, Membership Plunge Part of Stormy Past." *Birmingham-Post Herald* (February 17, 1990).

INDEX

• • • • • •